TRANSIT COOPERATIVE RESEARCH PROGRAM

Report 55

Guidelines for Enhancing Suburban Mobility Using Public Transportation

URBITRAN ASSOCIATES, INC.
New York, NY

in association with

MULTISYSTEMS, INC.
Cambridge, MA

SG ASSOCIATES, INC.
Annandale, VA

and

ROBERT CERVERO
Berkeley, CA

Subject Areas

Planning and Administration
Public Transit

Research Sponsored by the Federal Transit Administration in Cooperation with the Transit Development Corporation

TRANSPORTATION RESEARCH BOARD
NATIONAL RESEARCH COUNCIL

NATIONAL ACADEMY PRESS
Washington, D.C. 1999

TRANSIT COOPERATIVE RESEARCH PROGRAM

The nation's growth and the need to meet mobility, environmental, and energy objectives place demands on public transit systems. Current systems, some of which are old and in need of upgrading, must expand service area, increase service frequency, and improve efficiency to serve these demands. Research is necessary to solve operating problems, to adapt appropriate new technologies from other industries, and to introduce innovations into the transit industry. The Transit Cooperative Research Program (TCRP) serves as one of the principal means by which the transit industry can develop innovative near-term solutions to meet demands placed on it.

The need for TCRP was originally identified in *TRB Special Report 213—Research for Public Transit: New Directions,* published in 1987 and based on a study sponsored by the Urban Mass Transportation Administration—now the Federal Transit Administration (FTA). A report by the American Public Transit Association (APTA), *Transportation 2000,* also recognized the need for local, problem-solving research. TCRP, modeled after the longstanding and successful National Cooperative Highway Research Program, undertakes research and other technical activities in response to the needs of transit service providers. The scope of TCRP includes a variety of transit research fields including planning, service configuration, equipment, facilities, operations, human resources, maintenance, policy, and administrative practices.

TCRP was established under FTA sponsorship in July 1992. Proposed by the U.S. Department of Transportation, TCRP was authorized as part of the Intermodal Surface Transportation Efficiency Act of 1991 (ISTEA). On May 13, 1992, a memorandum agreement outlining TCRP operating procedures was executed by the three cooperating organizations: FTA, the National Academy of Sciences, acting through the Transportation Research Board (TRB); and the Transit Development Corporation, Inc. (TDC), a nonprofit educational and research organization established by APTA. TDC is responsible for forming the independent governing board, designated as the TCRP Oversight and Project Selection (TOPS) Committee.

Research problem statements for TCRP are solicited periodically but may be submitted to TRB by anyone at any time. It is the responsibility of the TOPS Committee to formulate the research program by identifying the highest priority projects. As part of the evaluation, the TOPS Committee defines funding levels and expected products.

Once selected, each project is assigned to an expert panel, appointed by the Transportation Research Board. The panels prepare project statements (requests for proposals), select contractors, and provide technical guidance and counsel throughout the life of the project. The process for developing research problem statements and selecting research agencies has been used by TRB in managing cooperative research programs since 1962. As in other TRB activities, TCRP project panels serve voluntarily without compensation.

Because research cannot have the desired impact if products fail to reach the intended audience, special emphasis is placed on disseminating TCRP results to the intended end users of the research: transit agencies, service providers, and suppliers. TRB provides a series of research reports, syntheses of transit practice, and other supporting material developed by TCRP research. APTA will arrange for workshops, training aids, field visits, and other activities to ensure that results are implemented by urban and rural transit industry practitioners.

The TCRP provides a forum where transit agencies can cooperatively address common operational problems. The TCRP results support and complement other ongoing transit research and training programs.

TCRP REPORT 55

Project B-6 FY'94
ISSN 1073-4872
ISBN 0-309-06612-3
Library of Congress Catalog Card No. 99-71387

© 1999 Transportation Research Board

Price $29.00

NOTICE

The project that is the subject of this report was a part of the Transit Cooperative Research Program conducted by the Transportation Research Board with the approval of the Governing Board of the National Research Council. Such approval reflects the Governing Board's judgment that the project concerned is appropriate with respect to both the purposes and resources of the National Research Council.

The members of the technical advisory panel selected to monitor this project and to review this report were chosen for recognized scholarly competence and with due consideration for the balance of disciplines appropriate to the project. The opinions and conclusions expressed or implied are those of the research agency that performed the research, and while they have been accepted as appropriate by the technical panel, they are not necessarily those of the Transportation Research Board, the National Research Council, the Transit Development Corporation, or the Federal Transit Administration of the U.S. Department of Transportation.

Each report is reviewed and accepted for publication by the technical panel according to procedures established and monitored by the Transportation Research Board Executive Committee and the Governing Board of the National Research Council.

Special Notice

The Transportation Research Board, the National Research Council, the Transit Development Corporation, and the Federal Transit Administration (sponsor of the Transit Cooperative Research Program) do not endorse products or manufacturers. Trade or manufacturers' names appear herein solely because they are considered essential to the clarity and completeness of the project reporting.

Published reports of the

TRANSIT COOPERATIVE RESEARCH PROGRAM

are available from:

Transportation Research Board
National Research Council
2101 Constitution Avenue, N.W.
Washington, D.C. 20418

and can be ordered through the Internet at
http://www.nas.edu/trb/index.html

Printed in the United States of America

FOREWORD

By Staff
Transportation Research
Board

These guidelines identify, assess, and document the current practices that transit operators use to enhance their bus networks to better serve suburban travel needs. Taking into consideration the range of environments implied by the term "suburb," the guidelines identify six types of suburban environments and the applicability of individual types of transit service to each. The guidelines provide information on modifications and improvements to the overall suburban transit framework, and information on support and complementary services to public transportation. There is discussion on transit center-based networks, express bus services, limited-stop routes, local area circulators, shuttle links, subscription buses, and vanpools. Operating techniques such as route deviation, point deviation, and demand-response services are also discussed. Included in the guidelines are 11 case studies. Using the information gathered from the case studies, the guidelines discuss each type of service, covering its description, applicability, performance range, and conditions of effectiveness. The intended audience includes transit planners, general managers, and project managers; transportation policy makers; and city and regional planners.

The impact of suburban development on America's transit industry has been dramatic. Where transit operators once had well-defined downtown cores and could provide radial networks that served them effectively, the environment now contains multiple origin/destination pairs. Some operators have adapted well, offering riders a "family of services" concept, such as local and express bus routes, crosstown services, demand-response community-based services, and ridesharing and vanpooling. Other suburban transit operators have not fared as well. The oldest form of public transit in suburban areas is radial commuter service supported by various feeder services. Because of the gradual dispersal of jobs to suburban centers over the last 30 years, there is a need to better link these radial services to suburban job and residential centers for both traditional commuters and reverse commuters. In order to improve effectiveness and provide greater mobility to their constituencies, transportation providers, public officials, and planners need to improve the connectivity of suburban transit services. Transit service providers need easy-to-use methodologies for analyzing changes. Improving connections between transit services would expand destination choice and reduce travel time, thereby contributing to improved mobility, productivity, and efficiency.

Urbitran Associates, Inc., in association with Multisystems, Inc.; SG Associates, Inc.; and Dr. Robert Cervero prepared the final report for TCRP Project B-6. To achieve the project objective of providing guidance to transit operators and regional policy makers on how to enhance suburban mobility through traditional and nontraditional services, the researchers conducted a comprehensive review of current practices related to improving transit connections. A detailed typology was developed to classify suburban areas. Based on the literature review and the detailed typology, case study sites were selected that reflect the diversity of suburban types. The guidelines were developed on the basis of on-site visits and interviews with 11 transit operators from the United States and Canada, supplemented by reports and data for a select number of additional suburban transit services contacted during the course of the research.

CONTENTS

1 SUMMARY

4 CHAPTER 1 Guidelines for Enhancing Suburban Mobility: Overview and Summary of Findings
Suburbanization and Mobility, 4
The Guidelines: An Overview, 6
    Study Purpose and Objectives, 6
    The Case Study Approach, 6
    Suburban Transit Services and Operating Environments, 7
    Classifying Suburban Public Transportation Services, 9
Summary of Findings: The Keys to Suburban Success, 11
Report Organization, 15

17 CHAPTER 2 Suburban Transit Services: The Planning Context
Planning for Suburban Transit Services, 17
Suburban Transit Services and Operating Environments, 17
Land-Use Strategies, 18
    Transit-Supportive Design Guidelines, 19
    TOD, 19
Regional Growth Management, 22
Marketing Suburban Transit Services, 23

26 CHAPTER 3 Actions to Modify and Improve the Overall Suburban Transit Framework
Establishing a Transit Centers Concept and Timed-Transfer Program, 26
    Description, 26
    Applicability, 26
    Performance Range, 27
    Conditions of Effectiveness, 29
Enhancing Line-Haul Services, 30
    Express Routes, 31
    Limited Routes, 36

38 CHAPTER 4 Circulators and Shuttles
Local Area Circulators, 38
    Fixed-Route Suburban Circulator Services, 38
    Route Deviation Suburban Circulator Services, 44
    Demand Response Suburban Circulator Services, 48
Shuttle Services, 53
    Rail Station to Employment Center Shuttles, 53
    Residence to Regional Bus or Rail Shuttles, 59
    Midday Employee Shuttles, 63

65 CHAPTER 5 Subscription Buses and Vanpools
Subscription Buses, 65
Vanpools, 66

68 CHAPTER 6 Summary: Lessons and Conclusions
What Has Worked?, 68
    Operating Environment, 68
    Markets, 68
    Cost Control, 68
    Vehicle Types, 69
    Linked Services, 69
    Service Innovations, 69
    Public-Private Cosponsorship, 70
What Hasn't Worked?, 70
Where to Go from Here: Future Directions, 70

72 BIBLIOGRAPHY

76 APPENDIX A Classifying Suburban Environments

COOPERATIVE RESEARCH PROGRAMS STAFF

ROBERT J. REILLY, *Director, Cooperative Research Programs*
STEPHEN J. ANDRLE, *Manager, Transit Cooperative Research Program*
GWEN CHISHOLM, *Senior Program Officer*
EILEEN P. DELANEY, *Managing Editor*
HILARY FREER, *Associate Editor*

PROJECT PANEL B-6

BRENDA CLAYBROOK, *Dallas Area Rapid Transit, Dallas, TX* (Chair)
SHELDON CRUM, *Carter Goble Associates, Columbia, SC*
RONALD DOWNING, *Washington Metropolitan Area Transit Authority*
LINDA K. HOWE, *University of California at Berkeley*
PATRISHA PIRAS, *San Lorenzo, CA*
PHYLLIS E. PODGORSKI, *Metra, Chicago, IL*
KENNETH O. STANLEY, *Honolulu, HI*
JOSEPH GOODMAN, *FTA Liaison Representative*
PETER SHAW, *TRB Liaison Representative*

AUTHOR ACKNOWLEDGMENTS

The research reported herein was performed under TCRP Project B-6 by Urbitran Associates, in association with Multisystems, SG Associates, and Dr. Robert Cervero. Urbitran was the prime contractor for this project.

David J. Sampson, Vice President, Urbitran Associates, was the principal investigator and major author of the report. Contributors from Multisystems included Dan Fleishman, Principal; Susan Bregnan, Associate; and Rick Halvorsen, Associate. SG Associates staff were Frank Speilberg, President, and Randall Farwell, Associate.

Dr. Robert Cervero of the University of California at Berkeley was a major contributor to the work effort and authored several sections of the final report. Design and layout of the report were created by Ron Vogel, Senior Art Director, Urbitran Associates.

Finally, the project team would like to thank the staff of each of the transit agencies, metropolitan planning organizations, and local governments who contributed their time and insights for the case studies used in this report.

GUIDELINES FOR ENHANCING SUBURBAN MOBILITY USING PUBLIC TRANSPORTATION

SUMMARY Improving suburban mobility is a difficult national challenge, which is particularly acute for transit. Suburban development has had several major implications on the provision of transit services:

- Suburban regions are larger than traditional cities and have significantly lower densities. This means greater travel distances for most trips, fewer origins and destinations within walking distance of any single route, and more vehicle miles traveled to serve activities than in urban settings.
- The greater setback of buildings from roadways means that more deviations off the primary route may be required.
- Unless there are a diversity of uses in a suburban area, demand will be heavily peaked, with peaks at different times of day depending on trip purpose. Thus, to maintain reasonable levels of service effectiveness, services may have to be adaptable to different route patterns and configurations.
- In suburban settings, there are frequently several agencies involved in provision of transit services, and coordination of services and policies becomes a key issue in improving mobility.

The differences cited above with regard to travel patterns, land-use arrangements, and institutions suggest that not only service but also evaluation criteria need to be tailored to the suburban setting.

To provide a level of consumer appeal competitive with the private automobile, planning for mobility in suburban areas must embrace the family or services concept. Options must be created that are responsive to narrow market segments and special conditions of effectiveness. The challenge is significant.

STUDY OBJECTIVES

Suburban bus service planning needs to reflect the specific needs, patterns, and concerns of each local area. The purpose of the *Guidelines* is to provide those planning and operating transit in the suburbs with information about the types of services being introduced, the relative effectiveness of the services, and their applicability to specific urban settings. The *Guidelines* identify, assess, systematize, and document the current practices that transit operators use to enhance their existing bus networks to better serve suburban travel needs.

The *Guidelines* are based on case studies developed from on-site visits and interviews of 11 transit operators from the United States and Canada, supplemented by pertinent reports and data for a select number of additional suburban transit services from other operators contacted during the course of the research.

SUBURBAN OPERATING ENVIRONMENTS

One of the first tasks was to identify the range of suburban environments and to identify to the extent possible how they influence travel patterns and the suitability of individual transit applications. Six types of suburban land-use environments were identified:

- Residential suburbs,
- Balanced, mixed-use suburbs,
- Suburban campuses,
- Edge cities,
- Suburban corridors, and
- Exurban corporate enclaves.

Each environment represents a distinct operating setting that poses unique challenges to America's public transit industry.

CLASSIFICATION OF SUBURBAN PUBLIC TRANSIT SERVICES

How does transit serve these environments? Based on a review of the 11 case studies and supporting materials from other operators, a classification scheme was developed for describing the range of transit applications identified. The classification scheme is as follows:

Actions to Modify and Improve the Overall Suburban Transit Framework

- Establishing a transit centers concept and timed-transfer program; and
- Enhancing line-haul services, express buses, and limited services.

Actions That Create Supporting/Complementary Services

- Internal, local area circulators;
- Shuttle links;
- Subscription buses; and
- Vanpools.

SUMMARY OF FINDINGS: KEYS TO SUBURBAN SUCCESS

The *Guidelines* provide useful policy insights regarding how future transit services might be designed to better serve suburban markets. Following are 12 key findings the researchers believe to be some of the common features of successful transit strategies introduced for serving suburban transit markets:

1. Develop services around focal points.
2. Operate along moderately dense suburban corridors. Connect land-use mixes that consist of all-day trip generators.
3. Serve transit's more traditional markets such as lower income, blue-collar neighborhoods.
4. Link suburban transit services, especially local circulators and shuttles, to the broader regional line-haul network.
5. Target markets appropriately.
6. Economize on expenses.
7. Adapt vehicle fleets to customer demand.
8. Creatively adapt transit service practices to the landscape.
9. Obtain private sector support.
10. Plan with the community.
11. Establish realistic goals, objectives, and standards.
12. Develop supportive policies, plans, and regulations.

CHAPTER 1

GUIDELINES FOR ENHANCING SUBURBAN MOBILITY: OVERVIEW AND SUMMARY OF FINDINGS

Improving suburban mobility is a difficult national challenge. For transit, the problem is particularly acute. Networks historically have been designed to serve downtowns and concentrated urban centers. Many are ill-suited for serving the lower density and dispersed travel patterns characteristic of suburban patterns of development.

Suburban traffic congestion has grown tremendously over the past two decades, and it has become the increasing focus of the transportation profession. Mobility planning in the 1990s has shifted from emphasizing the automobile to enhancing transit services and transportation demand management (TDM). With passage of the Intermodal Surface Transportation Efficiency Act (ISTEA), and its emphasis on intermodalism, and the Clean Air Act Amendments of 1990, the need for expanding public transportation options and increased cooperation between the public and private sectors has been heightened.

The impact of suburban development on America's transit industry has been dramatic. Where operators once had well-defined downtown cores and could provide radial networks that served them effectively, the environment now contains multiple centers, lower overall densities, and multiple origin/destination pairs. Some operators have adapted well, offering riders a "family of services" concept, such as local and express bus routes, crosstown services, demand response community-based services, and ridesharing and vanpooling. Transit operators have reached out to work with transportation management associations, local governments, and private employers in efforts to expand mobility choices and also to act as partners in meeting the needs of the community, including addressing the Clean Air Act requirements.

SUBURBANIZATION AND MOBILITY

During the 1980s, America's suburbs experienced a third wave of growth. The first wave of suburban development, which began earlier in the century, consisted largely of middle- and upper-income households leaving the urban core in search of more spacious living conditions. This was followed by a second wave, with retail businesses migrating outward closer to their customer base and locating along commercial strips, in regional shopping malls, and everywhere in between. Decentralization of jobs marked the third wave of growth.

As a result of these trends, many of today's suburbs feature the same activities found in traditional cities, though often spread over a much larger area. More Americans now are living, shopping, and working in lower density settings that are less and less conducive to transit riding.

Average residential and employment densities today are not only much lower than a decade or more ago, but trip origins and destinations are also far more spread out. Nationwide, the share of work trips both beginning and ending in the suburbs, for instance, increased from 38 percent in 1970 to 52 percent in 1990. Traditional commuting paths are being replaced by a patchwork of radial, crosstown, lateral, and reverse-direction travel. Increasingly, there is a mismatch between the geometry of traditional highway, bus, and rail networks, which mostly follow a hub-and-spoke pattern, and the geography of commuting, which seemingly moves in all directions. This has led to more circuitous trip making and increased suburban congestion.

Suburban development patterns have several implications on how transit services are provided:

- Unless there are a diversity of uses in an area, demand will be heavily peaked, and these peaks will be at different times of day. In a traditional central city, the mix of employment, retail, and service activity means that demand exists along a route throughout the day. In a suburban setting, an office park will have high employment-related peaks, whereas a shopping center will have midday and evening peaks. To maintain reasonable levels of service effectiveness, vehicles may need to operate quite different routes and service patterns at different times.
- Suburban regions encompass far more land area than traditional cities. For example, Washington, D.C., covers about 75 mi^2 (194.25 km^2), whereas suburban Fairfax County, Virginia, with a slightly larger population, is almost 400 mi^2 (1,036 km^2). Suburban densities are lower than those of traditional urban centers.
- The lower average densities of suburban areas means not only that fewer origins or destinations are within walking distance of any transit route but also that the distances

traveled between points, on average, are longer. In addition, the lack of an interconnected street system results in less direct routings and more vehicle miles traveled to serve activities than in urban settings (Figure 1).
- The greater setbacks of buildings from roadways means that more deviation off the primary route may be required (Figure 2).

In suburban settings, several agencies frequently are involved in providing transit services (e.g., the regional bus service, one or more local suburban area bus services, and, in some places, a rail operator). The service policies and fare structures of these multiple operators may or may not be coordinated. The degree of coordination often depends on the funding policies of the specific state or locality.

Differences in trip patterns and in spatial and institutional arrangements between the suburb and the traditional city suggest not only that transit services be tailored to the new conditions but also that the criteria used to plan and evaluate services be different.

Encouraging and facilitating transit use in suburban settings requires recognizing that the automobile dominates travel and that the attributes that contribute to its dominance must be considered when new services are being designed. These attributes should be considered in developing "conditions of effectiveness" for planning new services (e.g., the criteria that new services will need to consider in the planning process to ensure effectiveness). Consumer appeal is central to the ultimate success of these programs and thus must be central to the planning effort. The following attributes of consumer appeal need to be taken into account when considering mobility options to the automobile:

- Directness and comparative travel time;
- Comfort and service quality;
- Scheduling for convenience (e.g., flexibility, minimized transferring, connectivity);
- Pricing, including overall cost and simplification of payments; and
- Market coverage.

Figure 1. A moderate density suburb in Portland, Oregon, showing how the roadway network inhibits fixed-route transit service.

Figure 2. A corporate office campus in Dallas, Texas, set back from the street, is a typical example of suburban employment centers nationwide.

Transit planning must account for these and other factors and must respond with appropriate services and policies. For example, to be competitive with the private automobile, rail shuttles must be designed to (1) minimize travel time by ensuring well-timed connections; (2) provide these connections as effortlessly as possible with short walk distances, tight scheduling, and appropriate frequencies; (3) consider mechanisms for single pricing of the entire trip; and (4) provide a direct, comfortable link between the station and destination. Even with adherence to these quality-of-service criteria, planners and operators need to recognize that only a portion of the market will be served by any particular service option and that other types of action will likely be needed to meet the needs of other market segments.

Planning for mobility in suburban areas must embrace the family of services concept and segment markets in order to be successful. Options must be carefully delineated to reflect what is, in many cases, a narrow range of conditions of effectiveness. Operators and planners used to counting center-city oriented ridership in the hundreds and thousands per day need to be attuned to the special nature of many suburban services. Depending on local goals and objectives, options attracting as few as 30 to 50 trips per day, if tailored to meet very specific demands, may be considered successful; such is the case with many rail shuttle connections, community-based demand response feeders, and single run subscription buses to single employers/employment parks.

The challenges of making transit work in the suburbs are immense. Transit today finds itself competing with the automobile in suburban environments with extremely low densities, dispersed trip patterns, abundant free parking, and inhospitable walking environs. And, based on national statistics, transit is clearly losing the competition; its market share of commute trips has fallen from 6.4 percent in 1980 to 5.3 percent in 1990.

Clearly, short of massive new investments in transit, coupled with a fundamental policy shift toward the creation of transit-oriented suburban development, transit will never achieve the level of usage found in most central cities. Nevertheless, effective planning and promotion of a range of market-oriented services should help to capture a greater share of the suburban travel market and thereby help communities address their mobility and environmental concerns. This document is designed to provide assistance in this planning effort.

THE GUIDELINES: AN OVERVIEW

Study Purpose and Objectives

The task of creating effective public transportation in the suburbs presents significant challenges. Transit in the suburban market, a market characterized by generally lower densities and more diverse travel patterns than the traditional urban transit market, has evolved gradually over the past two decades. The range of travel movements is broad but generally is characterized by three distinct patterns: trips from the suburbs to the urban core, reverse commute trips from the urban core to the suburbs, and suburb-to-suburb movements. Transit operators and planners are constantly working to adapt fixed-route services that work in urban settings to the suburbs, testing new and more flexible concepts taken from experiences with paratransit services, and broadening horizons to embrace vanpooling and other transportation demand management (TDM) techniques previously considered outside the realm of traditional transit operations.

Suburban bus service planning needs to reflect the specific needs, patterns, and concerns of each local area. Those planning and operating transit in the suburbs, therefore, need to have at their disposal a clear understanding of the local setting and types of service options available. As transit services are being upgraded or expanded nationally in the suburbs in response to local issues and objectives, better information needs to be made available to local planners and operators about the types of services being introduced, the relative effectiveness of the services, and their applicability to specific suburban settings.

The *Guidelines* focus on suburb-to-suburb and intrasuburban travel. The dissemination of information and a better understanding of transit service options for these trips will help local operators and service planners to make more informed choices for local services.

The purpose of these Guidelines is to identify, assess, systematize, and document the current practices that transit operators use to enhance their existing bus networks to better serve suburban travel needs. The suburban service strategies featured in these *Guidelines* concentrate on service modifications and innovations designed to create more effective networks. The presence of a suburban bus network is presumed.

Through survey research and case studies, the *Guidelines* bring together information on the range of contemporary practices to identify the types of enhancement strategies that have been used in different suburban transit markets to integrate transit into overall mobility strategies.

These *Guidelines* are directed to agencies, operators, and public officials in suburban areas who are involved in both short- and long-range mobility planning. The *Guidelines* are intended to be instructive in helping to upgrade and improve existing services and to restructure services to address the needs of the suburban traveler.

The Case Study Approach

The *Guidelines* are based on case studies developed from on-site visits and interviews during 1995 of 11 transit operators from the United States and Canada, supplemented by pertinent reports and data for a select number of additional suburban transit services from other operators contacted during the course of the research (Figure 3). Principal among these additional operators were New Jersey Transit (NJ Transit); Norwalk Transit District (NTD), Norwalk, Connecticut; Long Island Bus (LIBus), New York; Suffolk County Transit, New York; and Westchester County, New York.

The case study locations were selected by the research team, project panel, and TCRP staff based on information collected from a broader mail-out and telephone interview process during the first phase of the research. After a mailing to 140 transit agencies in the United States and Canada, interviews were conducted with the approximately 50 transit operators who contacted the team and agreed to participate.

The *Guidelines* used to select the case studies included consideration of the following:

- Selection of a group that would cover the full spectrum of suburban delivery methods;
- Distribution of agencies to include both small/medium, and large systems;
- Selection of operators both with and without rail systems;
- Broad geographic representation;
- Opportunities at each site to investigate multiple suburban actions;
- Selection from among those who responded affirmatively to the initial interview and indicated an interest in further participation.

One other criterion was used in the selection process: Cases already covered in *TCRP Synthesis No. 14*, "Innovative Suburb-to-Suburb Transit Practices," were not to be included as case studies. The agencies included PACE Suburban Bus Division of RTA (PACE), Grand Rapids Area Transit Authority (GRATA), Ottawa-Carleton Regional Transit Commission (OC Transpo), and New Jersey Transit (NJ Transit).

Figure 3. Location of study sites investigated for this research project.

Case study visits varied from 1 to 3 days on-site. During the visit, topics covered planning and project initiation, operating and financial performance, public policy, private sector participation, land-use and demographic profiles, and other pertinent information and issues. The intent of each case study was to develop materials to document performance and to study it in context to identify factors either contributing to good performance or creating conditions for failure (Table 1).

The case study data formed the basis for the development of these *Guidelines,* including observations on performance, conditions of effectiveness, and other planning-related issues. Even though a detailed protocol was developed for the case studies and 1 to 3 days was spent at each location, what is clearly evident from the research is the lack of uniformity in the data collected and reported from site to site, the inability of some operators to track individual suburban services separately from their larger program, and the unavailability of a consistent database about the market. To the degree that supportive data are available, evidence suggesting the influences of these service strategies on operating performance is reviewed.

However, it should be cautioned, attributing performance improvements or declines to service changes is fraught with difficulties. This is partly because few of the 11 case site systems had consciously sought to conduct *before and after* evaluations of service changes. Thus, no control sites were established by transit agencies within the 11 case study areas, nor were before and after performance data systematically compiled beyond basic operating and financial performance data. Nevertheless, although the *Guidelines* established in this research can only draw inferences from the associations between changes in suburban transit services and operating performance, and the influence of particular suburban settings, doing so has allowed the researchers to identify and categorize all types of services, to develop expected performance ranges, and to identify factors that contribute to success or failure.

Suburban Transit Services and Operating Environments

The term suburb is a generic identification applied to the developed areas surrounding traditional urban centers, and it implies a homogeneous type of settlement uniformly characterized by single-family houses and condominiums, strip development and malls, and campus business settings. The term does not suitably reflect the true heterogeneity of these areas, evolving patterns of development, and changing demographics.

One of the first tasks in this research was to identify the range of suburban environments and to identify as far as possible how they influence travel patterns and the suitability of individual transit applications. Research led to identification of six types of suburban land-use environments across the United States:

TABLE 1 General Characteristics—Case Study Systems (U.S. Systems)

	Service Area Population	Fleet Size	PM Peak Buses	Annual Vehicle Miles	Annual Vehicle Hours	Annual Unlinked Passenger Trips (non-rail)
Broward County Division of Mass Transit, Ft. Lauderdale, FL	1,300,000	196	148	9,875,600	692,400	23,490,000
Central Costa County Transit Authority, Concord, CA	360,000	112	97	4,305,900	298,600	4,648,000
Dallas Area Rapid Transit, Dallas, TX	1,771,000	871	721	22,188,100	1,477,900	45,814,000
Fort Worth Transportation Authority, Fort Worth, TX	475,000	150	110	5,532,000	370,600	5,811,000
Lehigh and Northampton Transportation Authority, Allentown, PA	390,000	66	51	1,796,200	139,300	4,123,000
Metropolitan Transit Authority of Harris County, Houston, TX	2,172,000	1198	851	42,774,800	2,714,100	83,840,000
Riverside Transit Agency, Riverside, CA	1,508,318	63	47	3,347,200	204,800	5,350,000
San Diego Transit Corporation, San Diego, CA	1,400,000	339	266	14,390,900	1,119,000	35,709,000
Tidewater Regional Transit, Norfolk, VA	1,000,000	201	112	5,811,200	438,500	8,753,000
Tri-County Metropolitan Transportation District of Oregon, Portland OR	1,200,000	587	490	23,664,800	1,716,000	55,291,000

Source: National Transit Database, 1994

- Residential suburbs,
- Balanced mixed-use suburbs,
- Suburban campuses,
- Edge cities,
- Suburban corridors, and
- Exurban corporate enclaves.

Each of these environments represents a distinct operating setting that poses unique challenges to America's public transit industry. It was hoped that relating these environments to the case studies and services being offered in the suburbs would lead to conclusions about the challenges and opportunities associated with serving each of these operating environments. Appendix A provides a detailed discussion of the six operating environments and the methods used for classifying America's suburbs, which are summarized here.

Residential suburbs, which occupy much of suburbia's land mass, range from large-lot, single-family tract subdivisions to more compact settings with a mixture of housing stock (Figure 4).

Balanced suburbs typically feature a mixture of housing, employment, and commercial land uses (Figure 5).

Suburban campuses, which proliferated during the 1980s, mainly comprise office parks, industrial estates, and low-density business centers. Most are master-planned projects configured like university campuses. All the case study sites had some degree of suburban campus development (Figure 6).

Edge cities, the massive suburban downtowns that blossomed throughout metropolitan America in the 1980s, feature many of the same land-use mixes and sometimes match the employment densities of traditional downtowns (Figure 7). According to one study, there were 181 edge cities in late 1994. Commute modal splits by transit among edge city employees have been as high as 30 to 35 percent in metropolitan Washington, D.C. (Crystal City, Rosslyn, and Ballston, Virginia; Silver Spring, Maryland) and as low as 0.2 percent in the Troy/Big Beaver Road Area outside of Detroit, Michigan, and the Boca Raton/I-95 area in south Florida. As they mature, America's edge cities are increasingly being vacated by large corporations, with smaller companies taking

Figure 4. Residential suburbs—newly developed single-family homes in Riverside County, California.

Figure 6. Suburban office campuses—a suburban campus outside Dallas shows the difficulties that buses encounter in trying to obtain access.

their places. Edge Cities in the San Francisco area are shown in (Figure 8).

Suburban corridors differ from many of the other operating settings in that they are linearly configured, often made up of an assemblage of land uses aligned along an axial thoroughfare or freeway (Figure 9).

Exurban corporate enclaves, the last class of operating environment, is largely a 1990s phenomenon. Research has documented the leapfrogging of new commercial developments into favored corridors and exurban frontiers in many growing parts of the country. Examples abound: Bishop Ranch is a major exurban enclave located in suburban Contra Costa County, California (Figure 10). Chrysler moved its corporate headquarters to Auburn Hills 25 mi (40.23 km) north of downtown Detroit; Sears moved its merchandising division to Hoffman Estates, 37 mi (59.5 km) from downtown Chicago and 12 mi (19.31 km) farther out than Schaumburg, where much of the region's office space located during the 1980s; and J.C. Penny opened its new 2 million ft^2 (185,806 m^2) corporate headquarters in Plano, 35 mi (56.33 km) north of downtown Dallas.

Classifying Suburban Public Transportation Services

How does transit serve these environments? Based on a review of the 11 case studies and supporting materials from other operators regarding suburban public transportation delivery methods, a classification scheme was developed for describing the range of applications identified. The classification system for suburban service strategies used for these *Guidelines* concentrates on service modifications and innovations designed to create more effective networks. After having reviewed the experiences from the case studies and supplementary programs noted earlier, a classification scheme has been developed that defines two major categories of actions used to improve existing suburban networks.

Figure 5. Pleasant Hill, within the CCCTA service area, contains a mix of housing, office, and commercial uses, which are beginning to form a transit village.

Figure 7. Walnut Creek, California, an edge city in the suburban San Francisco area, located in Contra Costa County.

Figure 8. Edge cities in the San Francisco area. Source: Garreau, Edge Cities.

Actions to Modify and Improve the Overall Suburban Transit Framework

All the suburban areas studied in this project already have bus service provided in at least a portion of their local service areas. In some cases, the services are outward extensions of traditional urban core services; in other cases, the services are provided by an entirely new entity created solely to address suburban transit issues. What is important is to realize that the framework for the local bus network in most suburban areas has been in place for some time.

Suburban operators have sought ways to improve the overall design of their programs to foster better linkages and to create better alternatives to the single-occupant vehicle. *These actions represent the first step in mobility strategies of most suburban operators and are generally taken at a system level.* They include the following:

- Establishing a transit centers concept and timed-transfer program and
- Enhancing line-haul services, express buses, and limited services.

Actions That Create Supporting/ Complementary Services

The actions described above are those taken by an operator to ensure that the core program/network is operating effectively. The second set of actions represents those that create supporting or complementary actions. This group includes

Figure 9. A mixed-use suburban corridor along a major arterial in the Tidewater Transit District, Virginia.

Figure 10. Bishop Ranch, a 585-acre exurban enclave located in Contra Costa County, California.

those activities undertaken by transit operators to enhance and complete their network. These actions represent enhancements to the network—actions taken to meet localized needs, niche markets, low-density markets where fixed route services cannot be effective, and emerging markets outside the current fixed-route network. They can be operated as fixed routes, route deviation services, or demand response services in response to local issues and concerns. For the most part, these complementary actions are linked to the core network to create a coordinated program of services in the community. Featured among these actions are the following:

- Internal, local area circulators,
- Shuttle links,
- Subscription buses, and
- Vanpools.

Table 2 classifies, by transit system, each of the operating programs investigated for this research by the categories defined above.

SUMMARY OF FINDINGS: THE KEYS TO SUBURBAN SUCCESS

The *Guidelines* provide useful policy insights about how future transit services might be designed to better serve suburban markets. Clearly, conclusions based on the findings from about a dozen transit agencies risk oversimplifying matters, particularly given that transit's response to suburban growth is still largely embryonic and not documented in a systematic manner. However, some patterns were uncovered that provide useful guidance to those planning new services, whether they be core services forming the basic network of services provided or niche services aimed at meeting special/localized needs among smaller segments of the population.

This section outlines the key findings, what the researchers believe to be some of the common features of successful transit strategies introduced for serving suburban markets.

1. **Develop Services Around Focal Points**
   A distinguishing feature of the more successful suburban transit service strategies has been the servicing of *hubs*—that is, points that represent either concentrations of people or transit vehicles. A *people hub* is a large suburban employment center, like Bishop Ranch in Contra Costa County or the Texas Medical Center in Houston. A *transit hub* is a designated transit-transfer point, such as successfully defined and employed by Tidewater Regional Transit or park-and-ride terminuses operated by Houston METRO. Quite consistently, successful suburban transit services have focused on points where the concentration of activities generates relatively high ridership counts, allows for efficient routing, and eases the transfer process.

2. **Operate Along Moderately Dense Suburban Corridors: Connect Land-Use Mixes That Consist of All-Day Trip Generators**
   Suburbs present a rich mix of densities and land-use types, with transit services provided across a landscape featuring suburban downtowns and highly developed corridors as well as many low-density residential enclaves and developing, nearly rural fringe areas. The range of performance among routes serving these areas is equally large. The research findings support the long-held belief that compact, mixed-use development is a key determinant for introducing and sustaining healthy fixed-route transit services and therefore underscore the need to more carefully integrate land-use planning and transit service planning in coming years as a means of strengthening transit's presence in suburbia.

3. **Serve Transit's More Traditional Markets Such As Lower Income, Blue-Collar Neighborhoods**
   As the suburbs have matured, they have become increasingly diverse with respect to age, income, and employment classifications. Although the patterns of travel are more diverse and densities are lower in the suburbs, the profile and travel needs of the residents there largely mirror those of urban residents. As such, most transit services in the suburbs, and especially the

core services largely consisting of traditional fixed-route services, work best within the context of the traditional transit markets.

4. **Link Suburban Transit Services, Especially Local Circulators and Shuttles, to the Broader Regional Line-Haul Network**

   The most successful suburban services are those linked to transit centers and regional line-haul services. Routes serving regional rail stations are particularly successful, providing the link for central business district-oriented travel. Successful dial-a-ride and route-deviation services, which often are used to supplement the core network, work best when they operate within a limited territory and efficiently tie to mainline bus routes and rail lines. Operating strategies that combine these two elements can result in an effective network of flexibly routed services in low-density areas that are tied to lower-cost/higher-capacity fixed-route services in built-up areas.

5. **Target Markets Appropriately**

   There are many examples of suburban transit that successfully serves "choice" customers, most notably express shuttles and park-and-ride bus runs to large-scale employment centers, but these services are oriented to niche markets and have a greater chance for failure. Services targeted to choice riders succeed

TABLE 2 Classification of Programs by Service Type and System

	Express Bus	Limited Service	Fixed Route Circulator	Route Deviation Circulator	Demand Response Circulator	Rail Station to Employer Shuttle
Broward County Division of Mass Transit						
Margate				●		
Pembroke Pines				●		
Cooper City				●		
Central Costa County Transit Authority						
San Ramon Neighborhood Link			●			
Route 103 Walnut Creek Free Ride			●			
Route 104 Walnut Creek			●			
Route 960 Bishop Ranch						●
Route 991 Concord						●
Walnut Creek Flex Vans						
Bishop Ranch Lunch Shuttle						
Dallas Area Rapid Transit						
Route 134		●				
Route 133		●				
DART About					●	
Fort Worth Transportation Authority						
Vanpools						
Richmond Hills Rider Request				●		
Lake Worth DoorStep Direct				●		
Lehigh and Northhampton Transportation Authority						
WhirleyBird			●			
Friendship Express						
Shuttles (1,4,5)						
FWS/Palmer Industrial Vanpool						
Metropolitan Transportation Authority of Horns County						
Route 292	●					
Queenline Express						
Metrovan						
Galleria Midday Shuttle						
Greenspoint Midday Shuttle						
TC Flyer	●					
Riverside Transit Agency						
Perris/Route 30			●			
Moreno Valley						
Route 16						
The Inland Empire Connection (Rte 100)	●					
San Diego Transit Corporation						
El Cajon/Kearny Mesa Express	●					
El Cajon Dial-A-Ride					●	
Spring Valley Dial-A-Ride					●	
La Mesa Dial-A-Ride					●	
Sorrento Valley Coaster						●
Paradise Hills DART						
Mira Mesa DART						
Mid-City DART						
Rancho Bernardo DART						
Scripps Ranch DART						

only if they are appropriately supported and if they have an appropriate role to serve. Since choice riders would prefer to use their cars, highway congestion and high parking fees continue to be the most significant factors influencing transit choice. Without these factors, niche services have great difficulty in achieving success. Besides such environmental factors, which make the service competitive with the automobile, these services must have active private sector involvement as well as pubic financial support.

6. **Economize on Expenses**

   Given that suburban services invariably have lower productivities than their urban counterparts, operators recognize the need to keep the costs of these services down so that their overall cost per trip, generally the key measure of effectiveness, is reasonable and competitive with other services they offer. The most common strategy for cost containment is competitive contracting of services to private operators with significantly lower cost structures. Several transit agencies have worked in partnership with their operator unions to establish differential wage scales for nontraditional services, which provides a win-win situation for both. In other cases, services sponsored by the transit operator have been contracted to local communities, who then provide the service through

Fixed Route	Route Deviation	Demand Response	Midday Employee Shuttle	Subscription Bus	Vanpool	Service
						Broward County Division of Mass Transit
						Margate
						Pembroke Pines
						Cooper City
						Central Costa County Transit Authority
		●				San Ramon Neighborhood Link
						Route 103 Walnut Creek Free Ride
						Route 104 Walnut Creek
						Route 960 Bishop Ranch
						Route 991 Concord
						Walnut Creek Flex Vans
			●			Bishop Ranch Lunch Shuttle
						Dallas Area Rapid Transit
						Route 134
						Route 133
						DART About
						Fort Worth Transportation Authority
					●	Vanpools
						Richmond Hills Rider Request
						Lake Worth DoorStep Direct
						Lehigh and Northhampton Transportation Authority
						WhirleyBird
●		●				Friendship Express
						Shuttles (1,4,5)
				●		FWS/Palmer Industrial Vanpool
						Metropolitan Transportation Authority of Horns County
				●		Route 292
					●	Queenline Express
						Metrovan
			●			Galleria Midday Shuttle
			●			Greenspoint Midday Shuttle
						TC Flyer
						Riverside Transit Agency
●						Perris/Route 30
						Moreno Valley
						Route 16
						The Inland Empire Connection (Rte 100)
						San Diego Transit Corporation
						El Cajon/Kearny Mesa Express
						El Cajon Dial-A-Ride
						Spring Valley Dial-A-Ride
						La Mesa Dial-A-Ride
			●			Sorrento Valley Coaster
			●			Paradise Hills DART
			●			Mira Mesa DART
			●			Mid-City DART
			●			Rancho Bernardo DART
			●			Scripps Ranch DART

(continued on next page)

TABLE 2 (Continued)

	Express Bus	Limited Service	Fixed Route Circulator	Route Deviation Circulator	Demand Response Circulator	Rail Station to Employer Shuttle
Tidewater Regional Transit						
Maxi-Ride					●	
Tri-County Metropolitan Transportation District						
Milwaukie Circulator			●			
Route 151 Sunnyside			●		●	
Route 150 Sunnyside			●		●	
Willamette/Route 154			●			
ADDITIONAL SITES						
New Jersey Transit Corporation						
Lakewood Park and Ride Express	●					
Hackettstown Loop			●			
Mays Landing					●	
Northfield					●	
Absecon					●	
Centennial Avenue Shuttle						●
Convent Station Shuttle						●
Lawrence Flex-Route						
West Windsor Flex-Route						
East Gate Lunch Service						
Norwalk Transit District						
Merrit 7 Shuttle						●
Virgin Atlantic Shuttle						●
Connecticut Transit						
Shoreline East Shuttle						●
Suffolk County Transit						
Route 110 Clipper	●					
Connecticut Transit/Westchester County						
I-Bus	●					
Long Island Bus						
Nassau Hub Shuttle			●			

municipal departments at a lower cost. Finally, subscription vanpools have also been turned to as a cost-savings strategy, replacing more costly express bus and park-and-ride bus services in low-density suburban corridors.

7. **Adapt Vehicle Fleets to Customer Demand**

   In addition to using standard transit coaches on regular fixed routes, suburban operators need to diversify their fleets just as they need to diversify their services. Large, comfortable, over-the-road coaches have been essential in attracting choice riders on longer-haul express routes (Figure 11) whereas vans and minibuses have been the vehicle of choice for flexible services penetrating suburban residential communities, serving suburban downtowns, and providing shuttle services to regional rail systems.

8. **Creatively Adapt Transit Service Practices to the Landscape**

   Suburban transit services must be flexible to adapt to the divergent markets they serve. Operators need to use the full range of operating actions available to them, think creatively when seeking solutions, and link these solutions together into a cohesive transit network. Although middle- and high-density corridors and downtowns may be practical for traditional fixed-route services—possibly augmented by express services—where densities are very low, route deviation and door-to-door services are recognized as the only practical ways to provide the level of service and convenience that can compete with the automobile. Using all tools available, and acting as a "mobility manager" and not as a bus operator, is a hallmark of the most successful programs.

Figure 11. An over-the-road coach used to provide the Route 110 Clipper service in Suffolk County, New York.

Fixed Route	Route Deviation	Demand Response	Midday Employee Shuttle	Subscription Bus	Vanpool	
						Tidewater Regional Transit
						Maxi-Ride
						Tri-County Metropolitan Transportation District
						Milwaukie Circulator
						Route 151 Sunnyside
						Route 150 Sunnyside
						Willamette/Route 154
						ADDITIONAL SITES
						New Jersey Transit Corporation
						Lakewood Park and Ride Express
						Hackettstown Loop
						Mays Landing
						Northfield
		•				Absecon
		•				Centennial Avenue Shuttle
			•			Convent Station Shuttle
						Lawrence Flex-Route
						West Windsor Flex-Route
						East Gate Lunch Service
						Norwalk Transit District
						Merrit 7 Shuttle
						Virgin Atlantic Shuttle
						Connecticut Transit
						Shoreline East Shuttle
						Suffolk County Transit
						Route 110 Clipper
						Connecticut Transit/Westchester County
						I-Bus
						Long Island Bus
						Nassau Hub Shuttle

9. **Obtain Private Sector Support**
   Because of the inherent risks involve in providing suburban transit services, the greatest inroads in establishing new and successful services have been made when the public and private sectors have worked closely together. The private sector can support new service initiatives in many ways: direct financial support; participation in employee subsidy programs; marketing and outreach; and a comprehensive TDM program offering flex-time, guaranteed-ride home, and other complementary actions. This support is a key component for successful introduction of niche services to the choice rider for work trip services.

10. **Plan with the Community**
    The best services are those that are initiated by transit operators working closely with the local community (i.e., customers, local planners and policy makers, and the private sector). Services initiated in this manner achieve broad-based support, are more responsive to real rather than perceived mobility needs, and in general are more responsive to the local issues, problems, and needs they are intended to satisfy.

11. **Establish Realistic Goals, Objectives, and Standards**
    Suburban transit ridership and productivity levels, even among core routes in a network (as opposed to niche market services) typically are significantly lower than for their urban counterparts. Expectations need to be realistic, and appropriate standards for success need to be set before services are initiated.

12. **Develop Supportive Policies, Plans, and Regulations**
    Land-use policies that foster transit-friendly environments and transit-supportive densities (e.g., concentrated development around suburban hubs) will contribute to the success of public transportation in the suburbs (Figure 12). Parking fees, mandatory automobile-occupancy standards, and other regulatory efforts will also contribute to the immediate success of many projects, but such actions need to be integrated into a well-developed and coordinated land-use, transportation, and growth strategy in order to provide for longer-term success for transit as a key component. Integrated fare structures to create seamless travel also need to be encouraged, along with TDM strategies to complement transit and provide flexibility and choice for consumers.

REPORT ORGANIZATION

Chapter 1 has provided the background for this research, including a discussion of suburban mobility issues, the objec-

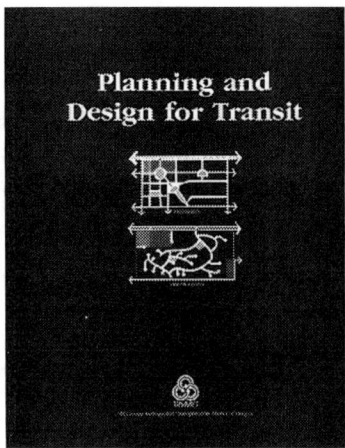

Figure 12. The cover of Planning and Design for Transit, guidelines for integrated land use and transportation development in Portland, Oregon.

tives of the project, and the case study approach. Furthermore, it has defined the classification scheme adopted for suburban transit strategies and presented a summary of the key findings taken from the research.

Chapter 2 places suburban transit development within the suburban planning context and identifies the relationships found in the case studies between suburban transit services and the operating environment. Specific strategies covered in some depth include transit-supportive guidelines, transit-oriented development, and regional growth management.

The next three chapters describe the suburban mobility strategies in detail, with information on specific services, performance levels, and applicability:

- Chapter 3 describes actions that modify and improve the overall suburban transit framework, including *transit centers* and *timed transfers, express buses,* and *limited services.*
- Chapter 4 describes experiences with *circulators* and *shuttles.*
- Chapter 5 describes *subscription bus* and *vanpool* programs.

Finally, Chapter 6 provides a synthesis of the findings, identifying what are believed to be some of the common features of successful as well as unsuccessful strategies introduced for serving suburban markets and future directions for continued research into this subject.

CHAPTER 2

SUBURBAN TRANSIT SERVICES: THE PLANNING CONTEXT

PLANNING FOR SUBURBAN TRANSIT SERVICES

The case studies reveal that the planning process used for designing suburban transit services is largely indistinguishable from traditional transit service planning. Most service planning takes place within the context of route-by-route performance evaluations carried out annually or semiannually as part of 5-year strategic plan updates. Routes are normally held against a performance standard, such as a minimum average number of revenue passengers per service hour. Poor performers are normally considered for either major service revisions or elimination.

New suburban services are normally instigated as part of a formal suburban service planning process. Once service options are proposed, designed, and evaluated, they are usually subjected to comprehensive review among stakeholders, including local transportation agencies and citizen interest groups. Other institutional forums were also introduced among the case study sites; some involved coordination among both public agencies and private organizations. An example is the Transpac (Transportation Partnerships and Cooperation) formed in Contra Costa County, a corporation that makes subregional transportation planning recommendations and promotes developing alternatives to private automobile travel.

Some transit agencies have carried out original research in designing suburban services. DART, for example, reviewed experiences with transit services in smaller communities across the United States to develop minimum population and employment density thresholds necessary to sustain various types of supply options.

SUBURBAN TRANSIT SERVICES AND OPERATING ENVIRONMENTS

In carrying out this research, the researchers identified six types of suburban land-use environments across the United States:

- Residential suburbs,
- Balanced mixed-use suburbs,
- Suburban campuses,
- Edge cities,
- Suburban corridors, and
- Exurban corporate enclaves.

Each represents a distinct operating setting that poses unique challenges to America's public transit industry. Appendix A discusses each of these six operating environments and the methods used in this research report for classifying America's suburbs.

Table 3 presents a matrix that cross-tabulates the different types of suburban service strategies reviewed in this report that have been applied to each of the six land-use environments. Several patterns are revealed by the matrix. The more traditional suburban settings—residential suburbs, mixed-use suburbs, and suburban campuses—have generally received the greatest variety of transit service strategies. Circulators and line-haul enhancements, in particular, have been concentrated in these settings. This likely reflects the fact that traditional suburban settings provide a more established and stable ridership base for designing and sustaining reasonably successful suburban services.

More flexible service options—route deviation and demand-responsive services—have been targeted predominantly at residential suburban markets. *Residential suburbs* also usually represent one end (the origin) of feeder links to rail stations and transit hubs. The reliance on more flexible and feeder types of services to accommodate residential markets reflects both the low densities and choice-rider characteristics of these markets.

Balanced, mixed-use suburbs have received very comparable suburban services as predominantly residential suburbs. In general, the market characteristics of these two settings appear to be similar enough that the same types of service offerings are provided.

Suburban campuses, like office parks, have likewise received a breadth of line-haul enhancements, like express routes to rail hubs, and supportive services, like midday runs between the campuses and nearby shopping centers. These more specialized services tend to rely on small vehicles (e.g., bubble-top vans), operate during limited hours, and cost nothing to eligible employees.

The types of services targeted at *edge cities* have largely paralleled those introduced to large-scale suburban campuses, with a few exceptions (e.g., circumferential services in Houston). In both of these instances, it has been the concentration of thousands of workers, regardless of whether they are spread out in campuses or contained in mid-rise buildings, that has given rise to these specialized transit services.

TABLE 3 Matrix of Suburban Transit Service Strategies and Land-Use Environments

	Residential Suburbs	Balanced Mixed-Use Suburbs	Suburban Campuses	Edge Cities	Suburban Corridors	Exurban Enclaves
Modifications to the Overall Framework						
Transit Centers	●	●	●	●	●	
Express Routes	●	●	●	●	●	●
Limited Routes			●	●	●	●
Actions Creating Complementary or Supporting Services						
Fixed Route Circulators	●	●	●	●		
Route Deviation Circulators	●	●				
Demand Response Circulators	●	●				
Rail Station to Employment Shuttles			●	●	●	●
Residence to Bus/Rail Shuttle: Fixed Route	●	●				
Residence to Bus/Rail Shuttle: Route Deviation	●					
Residence to Bus/Rail Shuttle: Demand Response	●					
Midday Employee Shuttles			●	●		●
Subscription Bus	●	●	●	●		●
Vanpools	●	●	●			

Moreover, transit services tailored to office parks and edges cities have also been spawned by mandatory trip reduction ordinances and TDM requirements. It has been in large part the critical masses of workers and institutional support from large companies that have helped sustain specialized feeder and shuttle services to large employment centers.

To date, *suburban corridors* have received both direct express and circumferentially configured bus services. Among the case sites, most suburban-corridor examples are in the Houston area. In cases of *exurban corporate enclaves,* like Plano north of Dallas (Figure 13) and the Woodlands north of Houston, express, crosstown bus connections from either residential neighborhoods or park-and-ride lots have been relied upon to serve these markets. The most ambitious transit program to date targeted at an exurban enclave is found not among the case sites but in the Chicago region, where PACE has introduced nearly 100 subscription vans to serve the new Sears merchandising center headquarters in the community of Hoffman Estates. The program has been highly successful, with around 30 percent of Sears's 5000 suburban workers currently commuting by some form of mass transit, compared with around 6 percent of suburban/exurban workers who transit-commute for the Chicago region at large.

Overall, the case studies provide glimpses into which service strategies work best in which kinds of operating environment settings. Low-density, single-use settings—like residential suburbs and suburban campuses—tend to receive point-to-point services, with buses often tying into a transfer hub or rail station, or else demand responsive services. Mixed-use suburbs and edge cities, because of their higher average densities and variety of activities, tend to receive both these as well as more specialized services (e.g., noontime shuttles) that are usually integrated into timed-transfer networks. Beyond these generalizations, however, it is apparent that considerable knowledge gaps remain regarding the relative success at adapting suburban transit services to different land-use environments. This is an area in which consideration should be given to targeting future research efforts.

LAND-USE STRATEGIES

Three different types of land-use strategies have been introduced as tools for promoting transit ridership in suburban settings: (1) development of transit-supportive design guidelines; (2) planning and formation of transit-oriented development (TOD); and (3) regional growth management. These strategies have sought to create built forms that are conducive to transit riding at three different grains of development. Design guidelines have focused at the site level, seeking to promote suburban designs that both facilitate walking access to transit stops and allow for efficient transit vehicular movements. TOD initiatives, on the other hand, have generally been

Figure 13. DART Crosstown Limited bus services providing service to office parks in Plano, Texas.

directed at the *community* level, aiming to create suburban neighborhoods that are compact, mixed-use, and pedestrian-friendly within close proximity to rail stations and major bus transit stops. Regional growth management efforts have generally sought to influence urban form at a *regional* level, such as through defining urban growth boundaries that hem in new development.

Transit-Supportive Design Guidelines

A 1993 national survey found that about 25 percent of transit agencies in the United States have some form of transit-supportive design guidelines. In general, these guidelines promote the physical development of properties and sites (and, to a lesser degree, subdivisions and corridors) in a manner that supports transit services. Besides imparting technical design information, guidelines promote coordination among stakeholders, encourage long-range planning for transit, emphasize the importance of transit design considerations during project review, and educate the general public about transit issues. Some of the more effective guidelines provide examples of "good design practices" that developers can emulate.

Among the case study sites, CCCTA, Tri-Met, San Diego Transit, and BC Transit have strongly promoted transit-supportive site designs by widely disseminating design manuals (and in the case of San Diego, videotapes). In 1982, CCCTA published one of the nation's first transit-supportive design guidelines, *Coordination of Property Development and Improvements*. The document makes recommendations on the designs of residential subdivisions, roadways (e.g., geometrics), and transit facilities (e.g., siting of bus shelters). CCCTA's planning department has distributed the guidelines to areawide developers and other interests, hoping to promote transit-sensitive designs at the project conceptualization stage. Although CCCTA planners review and comment on all major development projects within the agency's service area, they have never tried to block a project for design reasons; they view their role simply as one of education rather than enforcement.

In the Portland region, Tri-Met has published *Planning and Design for Transit*. The manual describes the many virtues of transit-supportive development and presents examples of designing for pedestrian districts, zoning for land uses, and laying out on-site road systems. Figure 14 presents an example of how to appropriately design bus stop amenities, taken from Tri-Met's manual.

One of the most effective campaigns to date to promote transit-sensitive site designs has been undertaken by Snohomish County Transit, or SNO-TRANS, which serves sprawling Snohomish County north of Seattle. SNO-TRANS guidelines, *A Guide to Land Use and Public Transportation*, makes liberal use of graphics and illustrations and has gained national recognition as one of the best how-to guidelines for designing transit-friendly projects. Figure 15 presents an exhibit from the manual showing how, over time, a typical automobile-oriented suburban strip might be retrofitted into a more compact, mixed-use, transit-oriented community. Key to this conversion are up-front public improvements that improve the quality of the neighborhood and, as a result, help to jump-start private sector improvements. Several of SNO-TRANS's board members regularly meet with developers to review the manual and an accompanying videotape, and the board annually awards a prize to the county's most transit-friendly new development.

TOD

TOD has gained currency in recent years to describe places conducive to transit riding—compact, mixed-use communities that, by design, invite residents, workers, and shoppers to drive their cars less and use transit more. TODs embrace many of the design principles from traditional American towns like Princeton, New Jersey; Savannah, Georgia; and Annapolis, Maryland. Among the hallmarks of a neighborhood-scale TOD is a commercial transit-served core within walking distance of several thousand residents, a well-connected grid-like street network, narrow roads with curbside parking (to buffer pedestrians) and back-lot alleys, diverse land uses, and various styles and densities of housing.

Among the 11 case study sites, four stand out for their leadership in promoting suburban TOD—San Francisco's East Bay (CCCTA), San Diego, Portland (Tri-Met), and Vancouver (BC Transit). All have consciously sought to create a new form of suburban environment that in the long run could dramatically increase transit ridership.

San Francisco's East Bay

Within the service jurisdiction of CCCTA is the emerging transit village surrounding Bay Area Rapid Transit's (BART's) Pleasant Hill station. Between 1988 and 1993, over 1,800 housing units and 1.5 million ft^2 (0.14 million m^2) of class A office space were built within one-quarter mi (0.4 km) of the Pleasant Hill station. Pleasant Hill's success is attributable to three key factors: (a) the creation of a specific plan in the early 1980s that served as a blueprint for targeting growth near the rail station over the next 15 years; (b) the existence of a proactive redevelopment authority whose staff aggressively sought to implement the plan by assembling irregular parcels into developable parcels and issuing tax-exempt bond financing for public and private improvements; (c) having a local elected official who became the project's political champion, working tirelessly and participating in innumerable public hearings to shepherd the project through to implementation. Current plans call for converting two BART parking lots at the Pleasant Hill station into structured replacement parking in order to open up land for restaurants, retail shops, and a regional cultural complex, activities that are currently missing but are widely viewed as vital toward creating a more village-like atmosphere.

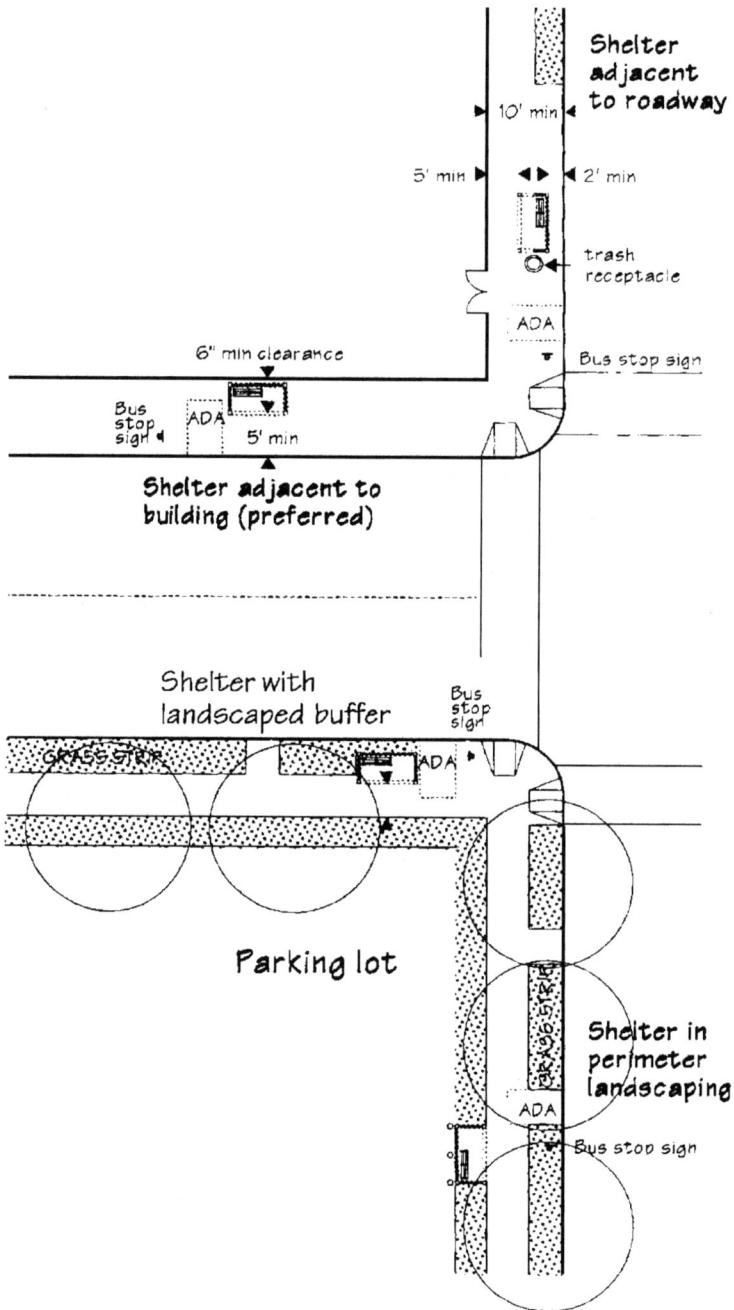

Figure 14. Designing bus stop amenities, one of the many guidelines provided by Tri-Met in Planning and Design for Transit.

Surveys of people living in Pleasant Hill's transit village reveal that 47 percent patronize some form of mass transit to work (either BART or the County Connection). This transit modal split is three times higher than for the entire city of Pleasant Hill and around five times higher than the Bay Area average. Tenants of the transit-oriented housing also own relatively fewer vehicles than the county average, in part because of the availability of BART and frequent CCCTA feeder services.

San Diego

In recent years, the city of San Diego has strongly promoted transit-oriented designs, adopting a formal policy "to direct growth into compact neighborhood patterns of development, where living and working environments are within walkable distances of transit systems" (City Council Policy 600–39). Since 1990, more than 380 modern apartment units have been built adjacent to the Amaya light-rail station in the

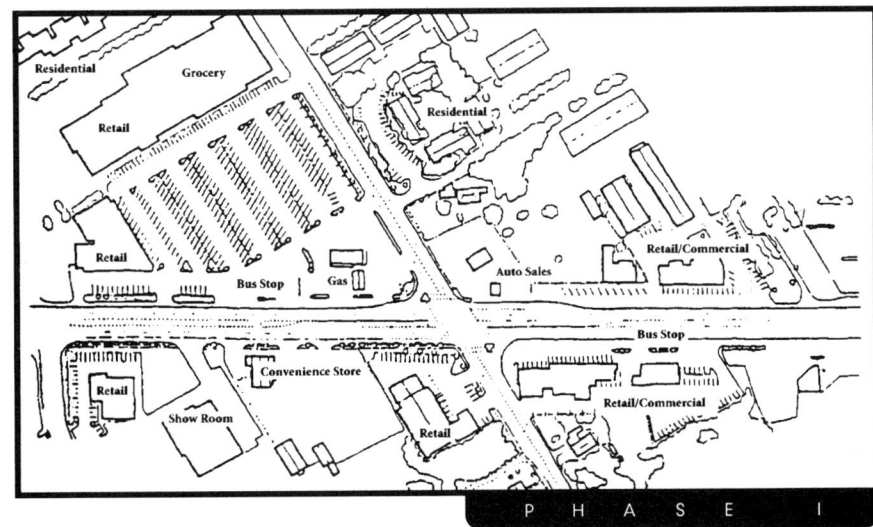
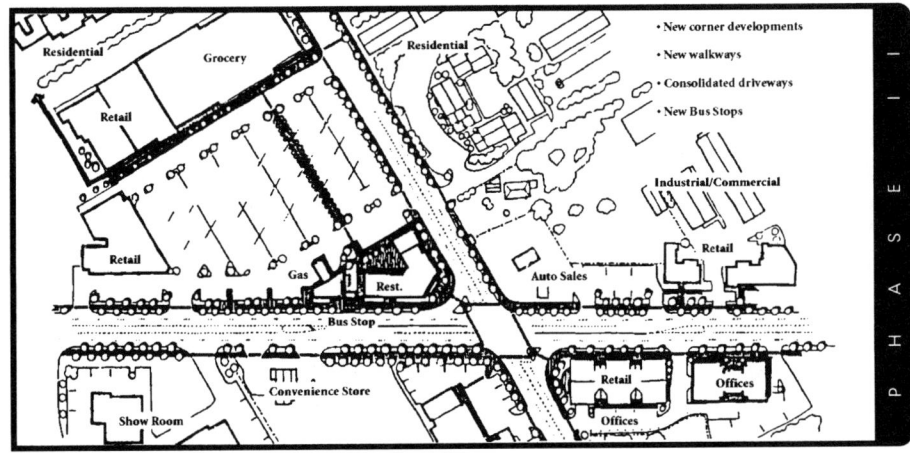
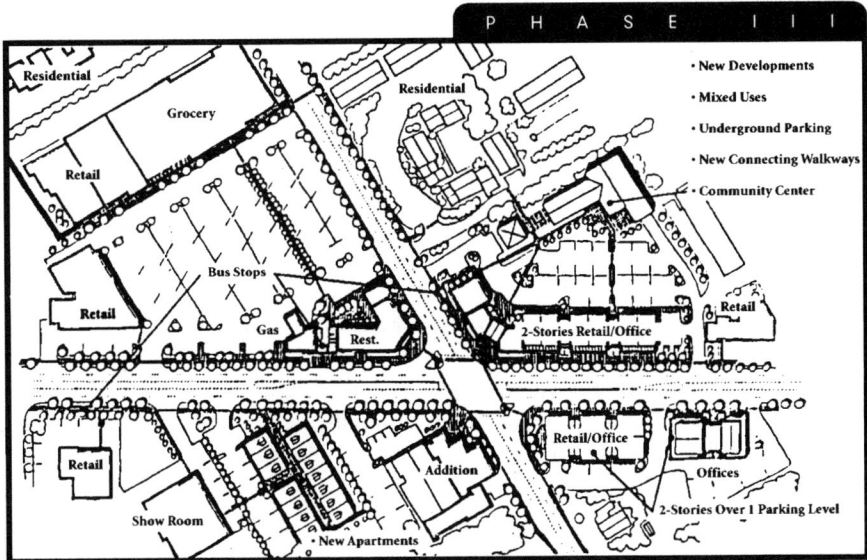

Figure 15. Automobile strip-to-transit conversion, in SNO-TRAN's Guide to Land Use and Public Transportation, Seattle, Washington.

San Diego suburb of La Mesa. Currently under construction is Otay Ranch, a master-planned community adjacent to the cities of San Diego and Chula Vista, which will feature five village clusters and will be served directly by an extension of the trolley line. The most ambitious TOD planning, however, is currently under way along the $240 million Mission Valley trolley line now under construction. Mission Valley has grown rapidly in recent years; it is the recipient of two regional shopping malls, several campus-style office parks, and San Diego's Jack Murphy Stadium. To effectively serve TOD, the Mission Valley crosses the San Diego River three times in order to serve site developments on the flat valley floors and preserve the sensitive hillsides that define the valley. Whereas earlier San Diego trolley lines were aligned along abandoned freight rail lines and freeway corridors to minimize land acquisition costs, San Diego officials have opted to align the Mission Valley corridor to maximize development potential, even if it means dramatically inflating the project's cost.

Portland, Oregon

Portland, Oregon, has gained a reputation as a national leader in promoting TOD. The MAX light-rail line is widely credited with stimulating redevelopment in downtown Portland and the Lloyd Center; however, to date little has happened along the east-side line that extends to the suburban community of Gresham. Portland planners hope to more effectively leverage transit, however, with the MAX extension currently under way on the city's west side. There, an ambitious, state-of-the-art planning campaign aims to create new transit-oriented communities that will obviate the need to build a planned west-side freeway. This western corridor in suburban Washington County has experienced phenomenal growth in recent years. During the 1980s, it accounted for two-thirds of population growth and 96 percent of employment growth in the Portland metropolitan area. Planning for this corridor has been a joint public-private endeavor. The region's governing body, Metro, in coordination with local and county governments, has led public sector planning. In parallel, the 1000 Friends of Oregon, an independent pro-environment group, carried out its own comprehensive planning, under the aegis of the LUTRAQ (land use, transportation, and air quality connection) program. The LUTRAQ study recently concluded that transit-oriented communities could accommodate 65 percent of new homes and 78 percent of new jobs in suburban Washington County.

Among the innovative planning measures currently under way along the west-side corridor has been the use of interim zoning to prevent land uses that might be incompatible with TOD during the planning stages. Besides prohibiting automobile-oriented uses within one-half mi (0.8 km) of planned stations, interim zoning sets minimum densities, limits parking supplies, and requires buildings to be physically oriented to light-rail station entrances. Additionally, public-private master development of transit-oriented communities, using some 1,500 acres (6.07 kms) of vacant land, is now breaking ground. One site, Beaverton Creek, located in the upscale suburb of Beaverton in the state's high-tech Silicon Forest, is slated to be the first project built under Portland's transit-oriented design guidelines. It is being planned by a team of landowners, including Specht Development, First Western Investments, U.S. Bank, Texktronix, and Tri-Met. The west-side line was routed to take advantage of Beaverton Creek's prime development parcel. Some 1,600 multifamily units at blended densities of 22 to 35 units per acre and several hundred single-family homes are proposed for the Beaverton Creek site. A generous system of pathways will also tie it to the Nike world headquarters, immediately to the north.

Vancouver, British Columbia

Since adopting the *Liveable Region Plan* in 1975, Vancouver has sought to create a system of town centers throughout the metropolitan area that would be efficiently linked by the SkyTrain advanced light-rail system and feeder transit services. The long-range plan calls for a hierarchy of urban centers, with the primary centers interconnected by rail and smaller centers relying on radial crosstown express services and feeder vans Figure 16. An example of transit-oriented development is the Burnaby Metrotown, an urban center that boasts a SkyTrain station in its core. Burnaby is a mature inner suburb of some 160,000 inhabitants located 6 mi (9.66 km) south of downtown Vancouver. In its transit-served core are moderate density commercial, office, and other mixed land uses. The core is surrounded by parks and a supporting ring of multifamily mid-rise apartments and townhouses. Single-family housing lies beyond the higher-density housing. This wedding-cake pattern of densities has put those most likely to ride transit— shoppers, office workers, and apartment dwellers—closest to the SkyTrain hub. Ninety percent of all commercial parking spaces in Burnaby are provided in structures or below ground. This has freed up land for parks, passageways, and bike paths that connect surrounding residential areas to the SkyTrain station.

REGIONAL GROWTH MANAGEMENT

Several of the case study areas also stand out for attempting to manage regional growth to create a more compact, transit-supportive urban form. Portland has long had one of the most ambitious regional planning and growth management efforts in North America. The Portland region has enacted an urban growth boundary (UGB). This boundary sets the outer limits for urban development over a 20-year period. Metro, the region's governing body, defined the UGB in 1979 and has made only minor revisions to it since then. The UGB's strength in containing sprawl will likely be tested

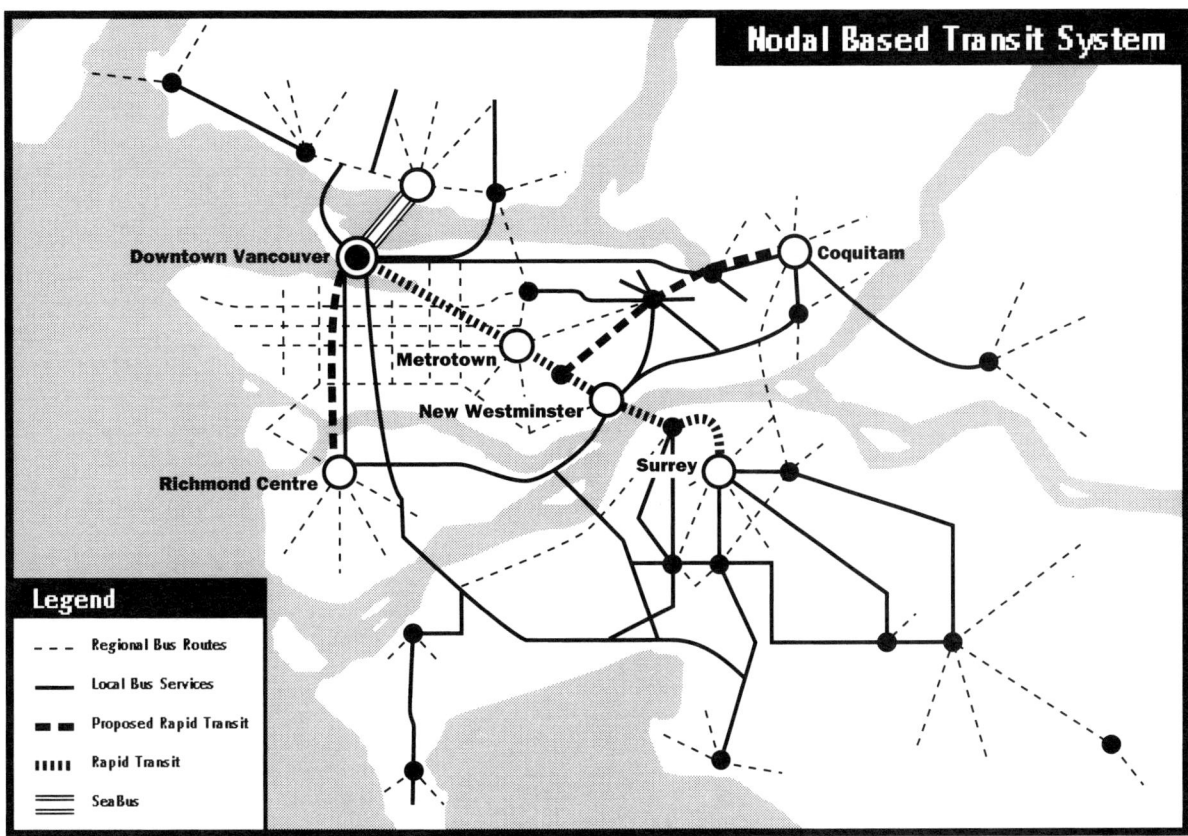

Figure 16. The long-range plan for the Vancouver, British Columbia, region links a hierarchy of urban centers using rail and bus services.

in coming years; it was originally drawn to contain a generous supply of land, and only recently have some cities begun to run out of developable land. To guide future growth, Metro has recently worked with local governments and citizens to reach a consensus on the region's future preferred settlement pattern in a process know as Region 2040. The adopted growth strategy calls for concentrating future growth in regional centers that are served by multimodal arteries and transit services (Figure 17). With an urban growth strategy now in place, the region has begun to move toward designing specific neighborhood plans, many of which are focused on rail transit stations.

Much of the impetus for regional growth management in the Portland region has come from the state of Oregon. In 1991, statewide legislation was passed that mandates implementation of transportation and land-use measures that will reduce per capita vehicle miles traveled in the Portland region by 10 percent in 20 years and by 20 percent in 30 years. This transportation planning rule has set into motion various initiatives to limit parking near rail stops, improve pedestrian and bicycle connections, and build more transit-oriented communities.

In the Greater Vancouver area, regional transportation-land-use planning and growth management can be traced back to the 1930s. The vision of compact and sustainable regional growth was crystallized in the region's historic *Liveable Region's Plan* that embraced the idea of connecting regional town centers by fast and efficient public transportation. As noted, these town centers have become the foci of higher-density development and the building blocks for a regional system of high-capacity transit linkages.

Last, the San Diego region has enacted a regional growth management strategy through the San Diego Association of Governments. The centerpiece of the regional growth management strategy is the development of reasonably self-contained, less automobile-dependent communities, like Mission Valley, that are conducive to transit riding.

MARKETING SUBURBAN TRANSIT SERVICES

Given the general unfamiliarity of many suburban residents and employees with nontraditional transit services, marketing takes on a particularly vital role in an suburban transit service program. As elsewhere, marketing has two key features: (a) identifying and targeting services to existing, potential, and emerging ridership markets; and (b) promoting and acquainting the public with service options.

Central city

Downtown Portland serves as the hub of business and cultural activity in the metropolitan region. It has the most intensive form of development for both housing and employment, with high-rise development common in the central business district. The role of downtown Portland as a center for finance and commerce, government, retail, tourism, and arts and entertainment will continue in the future.

Regional centers

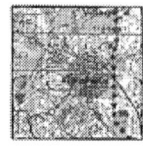
Regional centers are characterized by compact employment and housing development served by high-quality transit. Two- to four-story buildings are typical.

In the growth concept, nine regional centers serve six market areas – Gateway serves central Multnomah County; downtown Hillsboro serves the far western area; downtown Beaverton and Washington Square serve inner Washington County; the downtowns of Oregon City and Milwaukie along with Clackamas Town Center serve Clackamas County and parts of Portland; downtown Gresham serves the eastside; and downtown Vancouver, Wash., serves Clark County.

Regional centers are centers of commerce and local government services. They will become the focus of transit and highway improvements.

Corridors and main streets

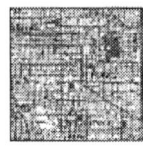
Similar to town centers, main streets have a traditional commercial identity but are on a smaller scale with a strong sense of neighborhood community. Examples include Southeast Hawthorne in Portland, the Lake Grove area in Lake Oswego and the Kenton area in North Portland. Corridors are major streets that are used intensively and serve as key transportation routes for people and goods. Examples of corridors include the Tualatin Valley Highway and 185th Avenue in Washington County, Powell Boulevard in Portland and Gresham, and McLoughlin Boulevard in Clackamas County. One- to three-story buildings are typical in corridors and main streets, and both are served extensively by transit.

Neighboring cities

Communities such as Sandy, Canby, Newberg and North Plains will be affected by Metro's decisions about managing the region's growth. While Metro cannot plan for these communities, a significant number of people live there, some of whom work in the metropolitan area. Cooperation among Metro and these communities is critical to address common transportation and land-use issues.

Figure 17. Development guideline examples taken from the Portland, Oregon, area's Region 2040 plan.

Figure 18. A CCCTA one-stop transit shopping center.

Figure 19. The Riverside, California, intermodal center showing the RTA information center.

Identification and evaluation of suburban transit markets are normally carried out through formal surveys, focus groups, and meetings with regional stakeholders and informants. Less formal approaches are also sometimes used. For example, transit managers often meet with drivers to discuss ways of tailoring services to customer needs.

Once services are introduced, typical marketing approaches include direct mailings, distribution of fliers, advertising campaigns, and radio jingles. Some service providers have gone the extra distance to get the public to notice and try their new services. When the WhirlyBird Mall express shuttle service was introduced, LANTA had a costumed mascot at the mall and gave away promotional coloring books with coupons good for free rides and gifts from mall merchants. LANTA adds the special touch of sending patrons a birthday card and free ride coupon when they turn 65. In Contra Costa County, new shuttles services were aggressively marketed through newspaper stories, television coverage, circulating brochures, and hanging banners along shuttle routes. CCCTA also considers its "one-stop transit shopping center" to be an important feature of its marketing campaign (Figure 18). Open from 6 AM to 7 PM on weekdays, the Center provides full customer information and services, including personal and automated trip planning, multiride punch cards and regional transit connection discount cards, and telephone information.

Where services are directed at specific residential neighborhoods, marketing has tended to be more targeted (Figure 19). The Fort Worth T mailed information packages describing the Rider Request component of route-deviation services, along with a refrigerator magnet listing the reservation telephone number.

To make their services stand out, several suburban transit agencies have also introduced unique color schemes. LANTA uses a special color and logo to distinguish shuttles from core bus services. CCCTA similarly uses a distinctive logo and color scheme for its shoppers' shuttle in downtown Walnut Creek.

CHAPTER 3

ACTIONS TO MODIFY AND IMPROVE THE OVERALL SUBURBAN TRANSIT FRAMEWORK

This chapter describes strategies used by suburban operators to enhance the performance of their overall network—transit centers and timed transfers, express bus routes, and limited-stop services. The sections describing each of the strategies, for this chapter as well as for each succeeding chapter, are divided as follows:

- Description,
- Applicability,
- Performance range, and
- Conditions of effectiveness.

ESTABLISHING A TRANSIT CENTERS CONCEPT AND TIMED-TRANSFER PROGRAM

Description

One of the most common types of changes introduced on a regional basis for improving suburban transit services is the introduction of timed-transfer systems organized around suburban transit centers. In metropolitan areas with rail services, these centers are very often intermodal terminals located at rail stations, supplemented by other centers located at malls, in suburban downtowns, or at other key activity centers. In non-rail cities, the transfer terminals are also often associated with the malls and suburban downtowns, and commonly offer transfers to urban bus routes to provide for regional trip making. The experience of Tidewater Transit, however, demonstrates that transfer centers can also exist independently of activity nodes.

Timed-transfer systems organized around transit centers are designed to facilitate transfers and reduce the length of waits. Timed transfers are particularly important in suburban settings because low-density operating environments often result in relatively long headways. Transit centers, ranging from the simple shelters of the Tidewater Transit District to enclosed, temperature-controlled structures such as in Dallas, serve as the intermodal hubs where suburban transfers are made (Figures 20 and 21).

Applicability

One national survey of 88 U.S. transit properties found that 68 percent of the surveyed agencies had some form of timed-transfer and transit center services; among properties with more than 350 vehicles, almost 90 percent used timed transfers.

Among the 11 case sites the researchers examined, two general approaches to designing timed-transfer networks were found, pulsed, and coordinated.

- Pulsed systems involve designing suburban transit routes so that buses arrive and depart transit centers at approximately the same time. Often a "window" is set where buses are to arrive within 3 to 5 min of each other. This means buses fan out from a designated transit center into different neighborhoods at roughly the same time and feed back into the same center at approximately the same time. A prime example of a pulsed system is Tidewater Regional Transit (TRT). Among the 11 case sites, TRT's timed-transfer system is the most impressive. Using Edmonton's seminal timed-transfer system as a model, TRT introduced 13 direct transfer centers in 1989. These are locations where buses serving two or more routes arrive within 3 min of each other. (Buses operate on 30-min intervals, normally scheduled to arrive at centers 15 min before and after the hour.) A 3-min wait time is scheduled at each location (with up to a 2-min extension if a driver sends a radio message that he or she is running late).
- Coordinated timed-transfer systems tend to operate more loosely. Here, bus schedules are not strictly set with vehicles expected to arrive within a few minutes of each other. Rather, in view of the sometimes circuitous roadways found in low-density settings, efforts are made to bring buses together at a transit center within a more liberal time allotment, usually between 10 and 15 min. In the case of Portland Tri-Met's timed-transfer system, feeder buses tying into transit centers face tighter on-time requirements than other buses, and they have a window during which they can wait for a delayed trunk-line route (Figure 22). However, waits of 10 to 15 min to transfer between buses among Tri-Met's 15 transit centers are not uncommon.

Every one of the operators surveyed had at least some element of timed-transfer/transit centers within their overall framework, whether the concept was a simple as coordinated transfers between feeder routes and trunk routes at malls in

Figure 20. A very basic transit center design from the Tidewater Transit District in Norfolk, Virginia.

LANTA or as complex as the network of suburban transfer centers in large metropolitan areas such as Dallas, Tidewater, Houston, Portland, and Vancouver (BC). In the latter cases, major transfer terminals were developed to serve as hubs around the region for the confluence of local suburban bus services, local circulators and shuttles, central business district (CBD)-oriented radial bus and rail services.

Tidewater's direct transfer centers operate in a manner akin to the downtown "pulse points" found in many smaller cities. The difference is that there are multiple pulse points and they are located throughout the region. An important feature of TRT's direct transfer centers is that they are fairly modest, which has lowered capital costs and saved on ongoing maintenance. Because all connections are timed, passengers usually move directly from bus to bus. This means they need not wait at the center or if they do have to wait, it is for only a few minutes. In inclement weather, passengers are permitted to stay aboard buses until their connecting buses arrive. Because all transfer activity occurs when several buses are at the center, security is less of a problem, even during evening hours.

DART has oriented its service around 14 transit centers, most of which include a park-and-ride component (Figure 23). The transit center serves as the transfer point between feeder/distributor routes, express routes, and crosstown routes. Most facilities include an enclosed climate-controlled waiting room with off-street loading for up to 12 buses. Several transit stations will become rail stations when the new light-rail system expands into the suburbs.

LANTA adopted a 10-year strategic plan in 1993 to meet its changing needs and included a strong push toward new services in the suburban areas outside the urban core. Shuttles have been developed that are linked to suburban malls, where regular CBD-oriented bus services are available. Use of regional malls enhances the viability of the circulators for local travel and offers a linkage for suburb to CBD trips that otherwise would be too costly to provide with a single direct route (Figure 24). It also allows LANTA to keep its capital costs low and fosters participation from the mall developers.

CCCTA operates all of its fixed route buses into BART stations with a tie to BART timetables but not a true timed-transfer pattern. Bus-to-bus transfers are increasing, however, and CCCTA is beginning to concentrate on non-rail station transit centers in other areas of the county. The centers themselves are carefully designed to accommodate bus operations as well as to maximize customer comfort and convenience during the transfer process. The concept is further supported by transit-friendly regulations aimed at concentrating activities around these transit hubs and promoting the transit village concept. In general, BART has designed intermodal facilities to allow for efficient bus maneuvers into stations, to ensure safety, and to make transferring convenient. Within its stations, bus staging areas are designed to provide sufficient turning radii and layover facilities for buses, space for shuttles, and to prevent vehicle conflicts. The sawtooth boarding bay arrangement at most stations allows buses to pull in and out easily and has made buses more easily identifiable, thus expediting passenger transfers.

The transit environment in suburban areas is defined by diverse origin-destination patterns and moderate to low densities. Under these conditions, it is recognized that ubiquitous networks are impossible to provide and even moderate networks are costly to maintain unless the services can be organized and focused so that the diverse trip patterns can be concentrated and transit services appropriately organized. As the case studies demonstrate, the transfer centers concept is recognized as the most appropriate approach to addressing these issues. It is applicable across the board as a means of focusing services, linking local and regional systems in the most cost-effective manner, and linking the family of services needed to tailor transit to the suburban market. It enables operators to serve multiple origin-destination patterns more effectively and, through the use of timed transfers, to do so with a minimum of disruption to the customer.

Performance Range

Implementation of the first direct transfer centers in Tidewater in 1989 coincided with the first gain in system ridership after 4 years of steady decline. However, the specific influ-

Figure 21. A temperature-controlled suburban transit center in Dallas, Texas.

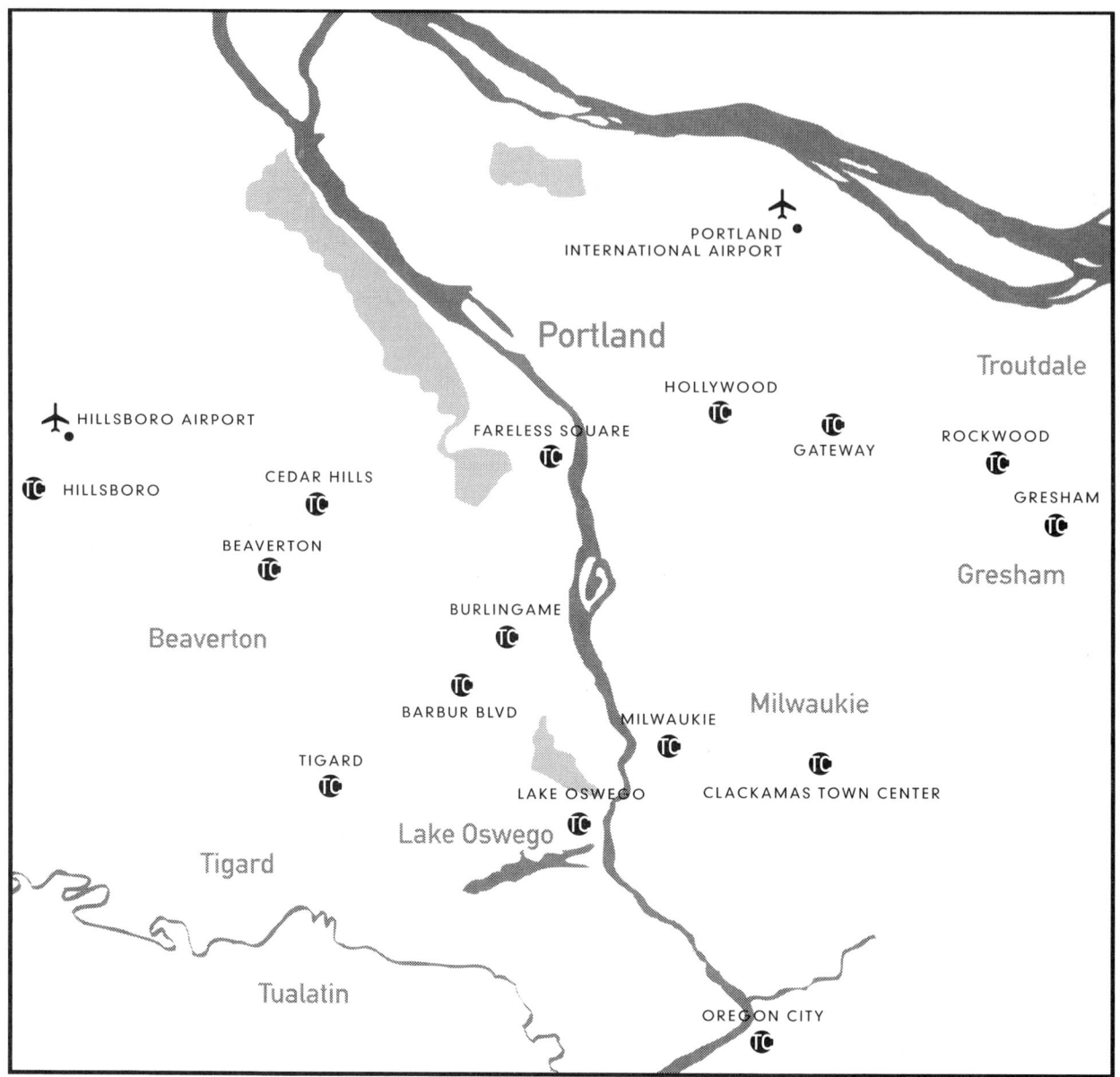

Figure 22. The network of transit centers for the Tri-Met transit system in Portland, Oregon.

ence of the direct transfer centers on these gains cannot be determined because other events occurred at the same time—elimination of direct service to some locations, provision of new services to other areas, and so forth. Moreover, the ridership gains immediately following the initiation of timed-transfer services were short lived. Ridership continued to fall throughout the Tidewater area during the first half of the 1990s in large part because of a downturn in the economy induced by defense industry cuts and deployment of naval personnel to the Middle East and other military locations. From a user's perspective, TRT's direct transfer system appears to have been well received. A 1992 on-board ridership survey revealed that three-quarters of TRT's customers preferred timed transfers to previous services.

More compelling evidence about the potential ridership benefits of timed transfers comes from AC Transit, serving the Oakland (East Bay) region of the San Francisco Bay Area. In the late-1980s, AC Transit began phasing in timed transfers in response to the suburbanization of employment. A multidestination transit centers program was formally initiated in early 1989. Table 4 shows that ridership increased during a 2-year period (1989–1991) when timed transfers and pulse scheduling were introduced within two subdistricts of AC Transit's service area. By contrast, patronage on the rest of AC Transit's service area, where traditional radial services remained, continued to fall over the same period. Service levels (vehicle miles of service per 1,000 households) were similar across the subdistricts over the 1989–1991 period.

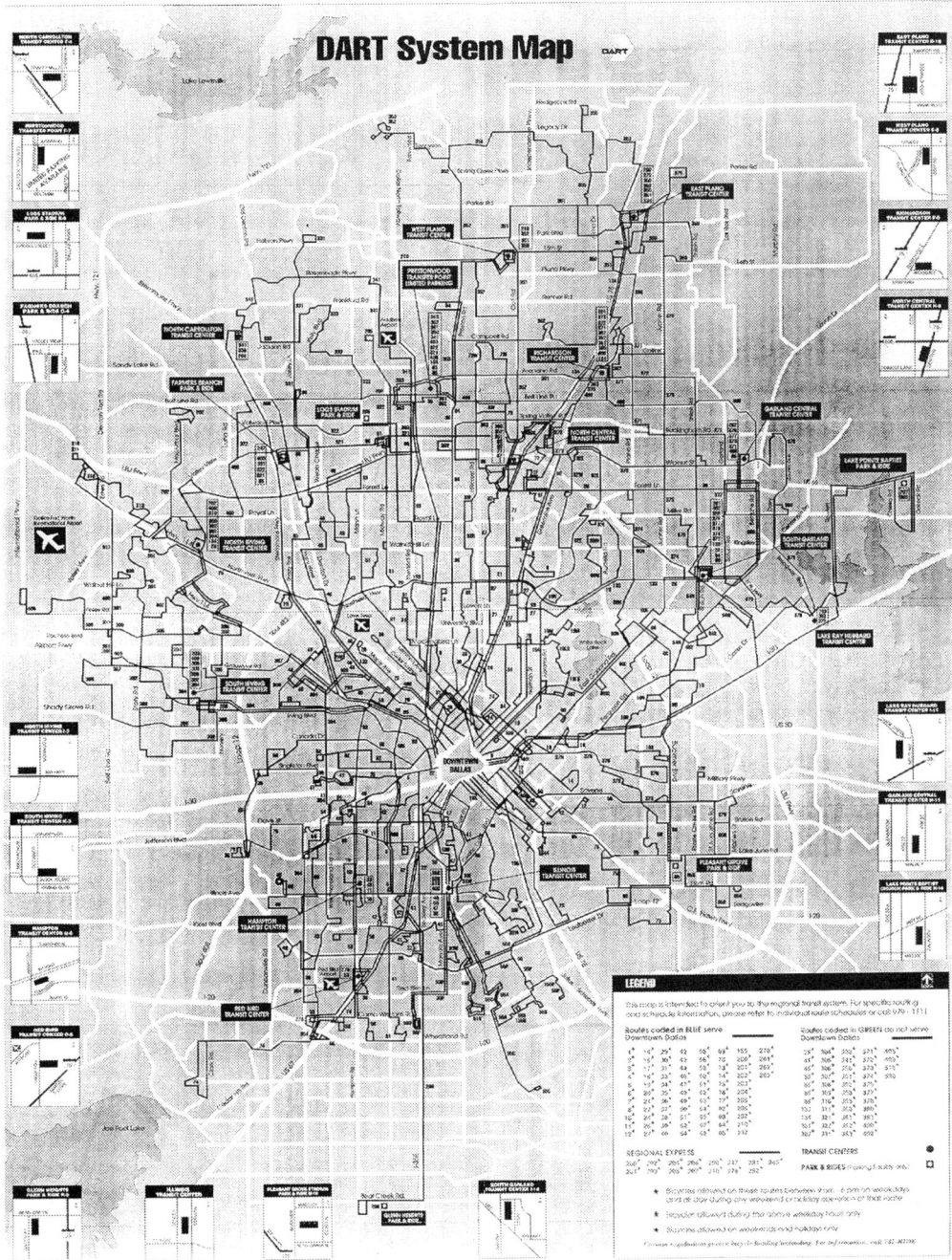

Figure 23. Layout of the DART timed-transfer bus systems.

Historic data from other areas also seem to indicate that the switch to timed transfers can have a positive impact on ridership. Comparisons of ridership 1 year after introduction of timed transfers showed systemwide increases of 3.2 percent in Dayton, Ohio (between 1990 and 1991), and 40 percent in Painsville, Ohio (between 1989 and 1990), even though ridership was falling for most other Ohio transit properties for the same periods.

In general, even in the absence of any quantitative data on performance, operators and customers generally agree that the timed-transfer concept provides mobility benefits to the customer and cost savings to the operator, albeit with a modest loss in directness for some origin-destination pairs.

Conditions of Effectiveness

The conditions of effectiveness are generally straightforward for implementing a transfer centers approach. They include the following:

Figure 24. A LANTA suburban transfer center located at the regional mall offers convenient transfers between local circulators and shuttles and the regional line-haul network.

- An overall strategy described in a long-range plan for the area can provide significant support in the development of a transfer center concept. Having a coordinated land-use/transportation strategy in place has provided the impetus for major initiatives in Vancouver (BC) and Dallas and supports the actions taken in Tidewater and Contra Costa County by fostering development strategies that will strengthen the concept. Plans with long-term commitments to transit-friendly designs, land-use controls to concentrate development around transit centers, and the like will continue to strengthen the impetus for transit center development.
- Establishing support among local planners and policy makers, developers, and mall owners helps to develop, design, and promote transit-friendly centers. Being allowed to develop centers at malls or other major activity centers (besides rail stations) enhances use of buses for both local and regional travel.
- Clearly, the presence of rail to serve as a hub for the transfer center concept helps immensely, providing a major impetus to local bus ridership. Strong connections to express buses and other CBD-bound services can have similar effects, especially if wait times are minimized.
- Not all arrivals at a transit center come by local bus for their transfer to rail or express bus. Parking lots at transit centers will encourage transit use for the line-haul trip even if it competes, locally with the feeder bus network. Although it is recognized that no level of bus service will attract everyone, park-and-ride lots will provide additional benefits to the community at large if a significant number of riders are persuaded to make their line-haul trip via transit and not on congested roadways (Figure 25).
- Because the concept tends to lengthen many trips by forcing routes into a transfer center, care needs to be taken to understand origin-destination patterns to avoid long bus trips compared with the same trip taken by car. The transit trip cannot be made so indirect that it becomes uncompetitive even for the nontransferring passenger.
- Although the transit center can be quite modest, constant attention is still required to keep it clean and attractive to users. Furthermore, riders need to feel safe and secure, which requires consideration of the center location as well as a plan for ongoing supervision of the site.
- Transfer fees, if any, need to be kept low to encourage these trips. Furthermore, low-cost or no-cost transfers should be allowed between various operators, with the ideal being a seamless fare approach that allows free movement among all operators using the transfer center.

ENHANCING LINE-HAUL SERVICES

The backbone of any bus system, urban or suburban, is its network of trunk-line routes. Suburban operators have found that, when properly planned and implemented, enhancing

TABLE 4 Ridership Trends Associated with Phase-In by AC Transit of Multidestination, Timed-transfer System, 1989–1991

Subdistrict	Average Weekly Ridership		% Change
	December 1989	December 1991	
West Contra Costa County[a]	12,488	28,329	+32
Oakland-Berkeley-Alameda[b]	146,386	156,987	+7
Remainder of AC Transit Service Area	58,671	49,357	-16
SYSTEM TOTAL	226,545	234,673	+4

[a] Multi-destination and timed transfer system introduced in September 1990
[b] Multi-destination and timed transfer system introduced in April 1991

Source: R. Cervero, "Making Transit Work in the Suburbs," Transportation Research Record 1451, pp. 3-11

Figure 25. Many of the Dallas transfer centers are located at park-and-ride facilities.

these local routes with limited-stop or express bus routes offering a higher quality of service can improve service for its core riders and can attract choice riders to the system. This section describes experiences with these two concepts for suburb-to-suburb travel.

Express Routes

For long distance trip making from suburb-to-suburb, particularly for commuter trips, many operators have begun express bus services, hoping to provide travel speeds similar to single-occupant vehicles coupled with comfort and reliability aimed at offering a stress-free ride.

Description

Express bus service generally consists of long-haul, moderate- to high-speed routes with few stops, serving regional trips. Stops, if any, are widely spaced, for collection and distribution, and most of the route is operated at high speeds along the arterial or highway network (Figure 26). Ideally, express services are provided with special equipment, which is designed for more comfort than regular coaches in local service.

There are a range of variations in the way express bus services are provided, but the underlying principal is to provide a higher speed, more comfortable ride than local bus service offers, so that public transportation can be competitive with the automobile for longer distance trips, particularly for commuter trips. Speed, reliability, and comfort are key determinants of the success of these services along with pricing and availability.

To obtain reliable travel times and competitive travel speeds, as much of the trip as possible is provided on highways or arterial roadways, preferably with special treatments such as bus or high-occupancy vehicle (HOV) lanes. Most

Figure 26. Cover art for route maps and schedules for two suburban express bus services.

frequently, these lanes are oriented to CBD-bound express buses, but the use of HOV lanes for suburb-to-suburb travel has been increasing and was cited in at least one of the case studies. To minimize in-vehicle travel times, express buses will originate at park-and-ride lots in some cases, with collection being done either by local buses or by automobile. Finally, operators increasingly have developed express bus services with special equipment, featuring cushioned seats, individual interior lighting, and other features to compete with the comforts of the automobile.

Applicability

There are two general applications of express bus services found among suburban operations.

Corridor Enhancement. Express bus services are used to offer a higher level of service in heavily traveled corridors, often to supplement local bus services running along the same corridor. These expresses often use the same roadways as the local buses, achieving higher operating speeds by reducing the number of stops along the route. To achieve higher speeds, selected sections of the routes can be operated along limited access highways instead of along the arterial road network.

Passengers boarding and alighting at the ends of existing local routes are provided with higher quality service, and at the same time loads on heavily traveled local buses can be reduced to acceptable levels. New riders are attracted by the faster travel speeds and, in many cases, more comfortable equipment used on the express buses.

Corridors in which suburb-to-suburb express services operate need to be densely developed with both significant numbers of residents and activity centers. Furthermore, they need to be anchored by well-defined, active terminal points upon which the service is oriented. In the case of the Inland Empire Express, operated by the Riverside Transit Agency, the two terminal locations are the Edge Cities of San Bernardino and Riverside, which are not only final destinations for many trips but also major transfer points to local Omnitrans and Riverside Transit buses.

Long Island Bus (LI Bus), which operates in suburban Nassau County and adjoins New York City on the east, has a number of high-density bus corridors that connect major suburban activity centers to the New York City subway network in Eastern Queens County. Once primarily oriented for Nassau residents going into New York, these corridors now have significant travel in both directions as employment opportunities have expanded to the suburbs. In recent planning studies, these corridors have been identified for the development of express bus and limited bus services, operated in much the same manner as described for the Inland Empire Express. The express services would operate between the terminals in Queens and those in Nassau County without interim stops; the limiteds would provide stops along the route at key activity nodes. LI Bus hopes to separate loads in this manner to operate more efficiently, thus improving overall operations, and to enhance its services to attract additional choice riders to transit.

In both cases, another factor in the application of express services is to offer a premium service, relative to a local bus, but at a fare lower than that of parallel rail services—Metrolink in Riverside County and Long Island Rail Road in Nassau County. The express buses and rail services, though both in the same corridor, have been found to attract different markets, with the bus riders generally having a lower income profile and shorter average trip lengths.

The frequency of the service and total trip length appear to be highly dependent on local conditions and markets. Riverside Transit operates Route 100 on 75-min headways, and the total route travel time is 35 min. As the next section on performance shows, despite the long headways, the route has good ridership. The LI Bus service, as described in the agency's recent planning study, could have as many as four to six express trips per hour interspersed with a local service operating as frequently as every 5 min.

Peak Employment Services. Express buses are used by a number of operators to offer entirely new commuter-oriented services to compete with the single-occupant vehicle in heavily congested corridors. Typically there are three to five trips in the peak direction during peak periods. To provide flexibility, operators often ensure that service extends to the shoulders of the peak and that midday travel needs are met with either one or two bus trips or an employee-sponsored guaranteed ride home/emergency service program. Early morning and late evening runs generally have very low productivities compared with the peak runs but have been shown to be important "safety nets" for drawing riders to these services.

Typical travel times are 30 to 60 min, but the range among the case studies was from 20 to nearly 90 min. The application is best suited to trips of at least 30 min on the express bus itself and only where the in-bus travel time can be competitive with the drive time by automobile. HOV lanes and priority treatments at tolls or exit ramps significantly increase the competitive edge of the bus over the single-occupant vehicle.

Among the peak-hour express services described in the case studies, three operate from park-and-ride lots and serve major suburban work sites. Collection, which is time consuming and costly to operate, is dependent on automobiles in each case. None of the park-and-ride lots is served by collector buses. The express buses do provide distribution and collection at the work trip end, but, for total travel times to be competitive with the automobile, most of the time must be spent in express operation on the highway. The Route 110 Clipper in Suffolk County operates in an HOV lane of the Long Island Expressway (Figure 27).

Houston METRO provides express crosstown services between several park-and-ride lots and outlying employment centers, the most significant of which is Route 292, which runs from the Westwood park-and-ride lot, located in a principally residential area to the Texas Medical Center (TMC), a massive suburban employment enclave with 3,000 workers. TMC was considered an excellent candidate for express crosstown services for several reasons: it is one of the few suburban locales with significant parking charges—$70 per month for a garage space, $55 per month for a surface lot, and $40 per month at service lots; it features on-street amenities like sidewalks, shelters, and skyway pedestrian connections between buildings; and most employers help underwrite the costs of employees' transit expenses.

One of the services, the I-Bus from Stamford, Connecticut, to White Plains, New York, operates between the centers of two edge cities as well as along the I-287 employment corridor (Figure 28). Access to the service can be made via other buses and rail services at intermodal centers in both cities or from several residential areas through which the bus passes before using I-95. This service, initiated in 1996, provides a transit link in a heavily traveled east-west highway corridor unserved by rail.

Range of Performance

Corridor Express Service. The sole corridor express service identified in the case studies was the Riverside Transit Agency Inland Express, which has a productivity of 38 passengers per trip on weekdays and 20 passengers per trip on Saturdays, which translates to 21.7 passengers per hour on weekdays and 14.4 on Saturdays. During peak hours, there is often standing-room-only. The cost recovery rate was 20 percent. In comparison, Riverside Transit's local fixed routes had a 1994–95 productivity of 26 passengers per hour, with a range from 3.7 to 37.9 passengers per hour. For developing

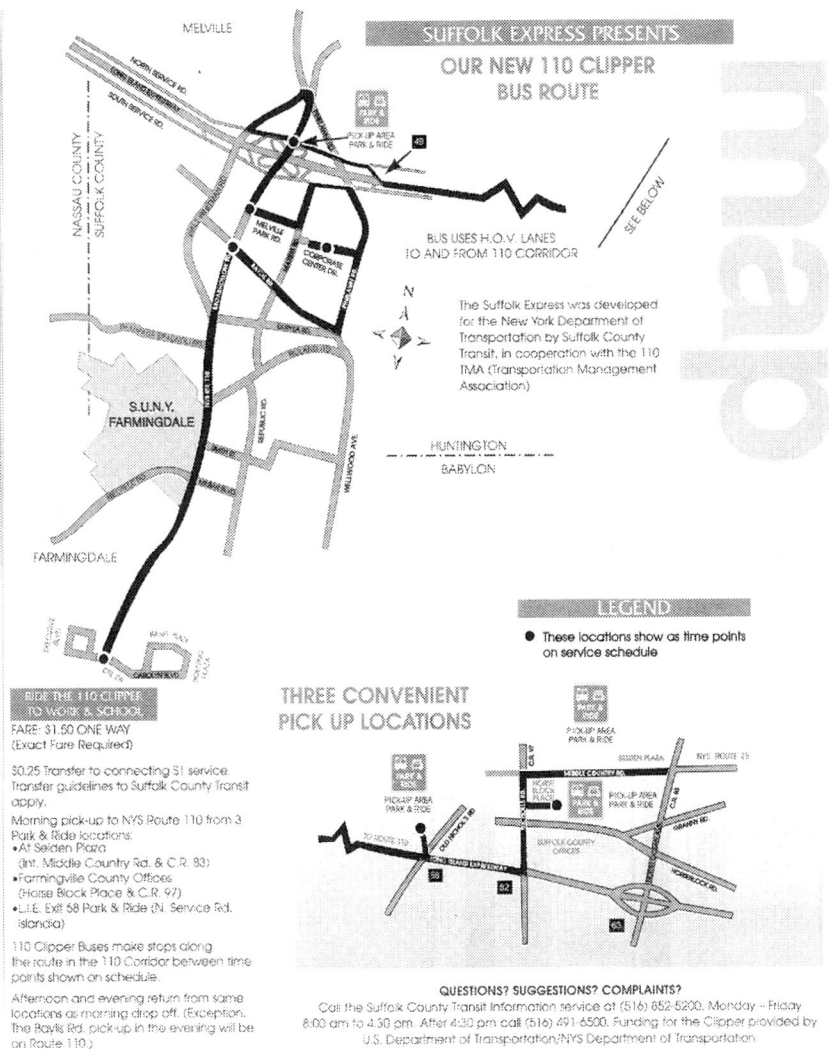

Figure 27. Route map and schedule of the Route 110 Clipper, Suffolk County, New York.

urban area routes, as designated by Riverside Transit, the average productivity in that period was 16.0 passengers per hour. The service also is considered a success in meeting regional mobility needs, as it strengthens the commitments to interregional cooperation, offers alternatives to transit-dependent populations unable to afford rail, and complements other fixed-route services.

Peak Commuter Express Service. The range of performance is large for the peak commuter express services surveyed for the project.

Introduced in fall 1994, Houston METRO Route 292 operates at 15-min peak-hour headways, similar to downtown express services. A daily ridership target of 648 was set for Route 292; however, after 1 year of service it was averaging only a little over 200 passengers daily. Follow-up surveys by METRO revealed part of the reason for this disappointing performance: many TMC employees were unaware of the service and the availability of employer-paid transit allowances. Several employees indicated they were not willing to "experiment" with transit because if they go back to driving, they would be placed at the bottom of the priority list for available parking spaces (i.e., they'll be assigned to the most remote parking space). METRO plans to continue supporting Route 292 and hopes to increase ridership through targeted marketing and working with TMC employers to change parking policies. METRO also anticipates trying new crosstown express routes in the future, most likely with contracted minibuses.

The Suffolk County, New York, Route 110 Clipper and Connecticut Transit/Westchester County (NY) I-Bus are relatively new services in their first year of operation. Each is generating approximately 10 to 11 persons per trip, with the Route 110 Clipper providing approximately 130 trips per day and the I-Bus approximately 180 trips per day. Both operators

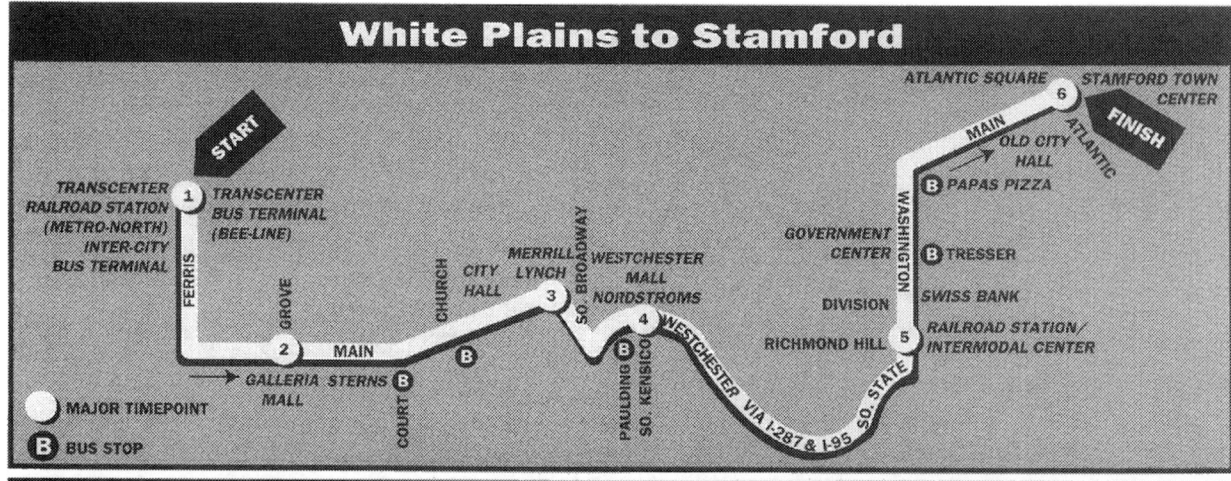

Figure 28. Route map and schedule of the I-Bus between White Plains, New York, and Stamford, Connecticut.

believe the services have started well and have potential for growth and will continue the projects for at least 2 years with CMAQ funding. The farebox recovery for the I-Bus was 16.6 percent. The Route 110 Clipper is operated by a private operator under contract to Suffolk County.

The last of the services included in this section is the Lakewood Park and Ride, operated by a private contractor for NJ Transit. The service, between two park-and-ride lots in southern Ocean County and the Lakewood Industrial Park, a medium-density employment location at the north end of the county, was discontinued after 2 years of operation because of poor performance. Before being discontinued, ridership levels were about three persons per trip, and the farebox recovery rate was 7.9 percent. The NJ Transit standard for their suburban service experiments is 25 percent after the second year. Elements contributing to poor performance were a lack of support from employers in the industrial park, no significant time savings for the buses on the Garden State Parkway operating in mixed traffic, and a dispersed residential marketshed from which to draw riders.

Conditions of Effectiveness

Clearly the range of performance indicates that a number of conditions that contribute to or detract from the opportunity to succeed with suburban express bus services.

Key contributing factors appear to be the following:

1. **Real employer support:** Although many projects are begun with the knowledge and interest of the private sector, in some cases supported by assurances of support, those projects with better records of accomplishment are those for which the private sector has contributed tangibly, with financial support either through direct subsidy or employee-subsidized passes and nonfinancial support with guaranteed ride home, flex-time, marketing and promotion, and so forth. The need for employer support is amplified for the peak-hour projects, which depend on commuters and specific employers, and less important for the all-day corridor routes, which serve a larger variety and generally more densely populated market. Planning projects with the private sector also contributes noticeably to success.

2. **Participatory planning and local support:** Projects that are planned with intended riders and/or sponsors have a greater record of success than those initiated and planned internally at a transit agency. Focus groups and surveys of riders; service planning with employers and projected riders; and participation among regional agencies, TMAs, or other groups are all actions taken to develop and promote new services.

3. **Congestion and parking fees that make automobile travel less attractive:** There is a direct correlation between ridership and the level of congestion and parking fees in the corridor for which the express service is planned. Route 292 in Houston capitalizes on the high cost of parking around the TMC; the Route 110 Clipper uses an HOV lane to bypass heavy congestion on the Long Island Expressway.

4. **High density destinations:** To obtain a reasonable level of ridership, given that even in the best corridors the transit share will be a fraction of the total travel market, there must be a sizable travel market from which to draw. Therefore, the destination for the express bus service must be reasonably populated and fairly compact—the number provides a base from which to draw, and the density allows the operator to provide reasonable distribution times that do not detract from the overall time savings achieved on the express portion of the trip.

5. **Reasonably populated residential marketsheds:** Similarly, the collection end of the service must have a reasonable population from which to draw riders. The origins can be served either by the bus itself operating in a collection mode, which works best in densely developed neighborhoods, or via park-and-ride lots in less dense areas.

6. **Bus priority treatments:** Bus priority treatments such as HOV lanes (Figure 29) or queue bypasses at entrances or toll booths allow express buses to save time over single-occupant vehicles, increasing the attraction of the bus service.

7. **Supportive regional planning:** Success often depends on the support of regional plans for transportation and economic development, policies that recognize transit as a tool for long-term regional viability, and establishment of reasonable program goals and objectives. Suburban transit service, taken as a whole, does not achieve the levels of productivity and cost-effectiveness associated with urban services; however, these services may contribute to regional goals for congestion reduction, air quality, and economic development. Although unreasonable costs are unwarranted, lower thresholds have been established in many areas for suburban services in recognition of their contributions to these other aspects associated with the "quality of life" in metropolitan areas.

8. **Transit-dependent populations:** The more successful express services are designed as much for the traditional transit-dependent markets as for the choice rider. Depending solely on choice users, in the absence of strict regulation or high parking fees and congestion, does not produce the volume of riders needed to support express bus service.

Figure 29. HOV lanes increase the attraction of express bus services in Long Island and San Diego.

9. **Special equipment:** Comfortable over-the-road coaches with special equipment—individual lighting, cushioned seats—are recognized as very important contributors to successful peak commuter express services, especially those that rely on the choice market for support.

Limited Routes

Description

Midway between local bus routes and express routes is the category of limited routes. Limiteds operate in much the same manner as the arterial expresses described above. They are used to offer a higher level of service in heavily traveled corridors, supplementing local bus services running along the same corridor. Limiteds use the same roadways as the local buses and achieve higher operating speeds by reducing the number of stops along the route. The M5 service in Manhattan, operated by the New York City Transit Authority, is an urban example of the savings that can be achieved between a local and limited service operating in the same arterial corridor. Along 5th Avenue from 57th Street to 14th Street in Midtown Manhattan, the local bus generally stops at every third block, or approximately 15 times; in the same section, the limited stops only 6 times. The travel time savings in this 2-mi (3.2-km) section, associated with fewer stops—including the time spent getting to and from the curb, signal delays, and loading and unloading—can be as much as 10 min. Passengers boarding and alighting at key stop locations are provided with higher quality service, and at the same time loads on heavily traveled local buses can be reduced to acceptable levels. New riders are attracted by the faster travel speeds.

Applicability

Corridors where limited services are applied need to be densely developed with both significant numbers of residents and multiple activity centers along the route. Local service needs to be fairly dense and well utilized to justify the additional level of service offered. Limited services require concentrated activities at key locations along the local route. If there are no concentrated stop locations along the local route, or if most of the trips being made are relatively short, then the limited service is not applicable to the route.

Only two suburban limited services, both from the Dallas area, were identified in the case studies. These routes provide limited-stop services to suburban employment centers. Route 134 connects transit centers in Plano, Richardson, Prestonwood, and North Irving, with local buses at each transit center serving as collectors/distributors. Route 133 connects the South Garland transit center to the medical area of Dallas. Route 134 was designed to provide reverse commute services from Irving toward Richardson and Plano. The routes were not established to supplement existing local services but rather to serve emerging patterns identified by planners.

As noted in the section on express buses, LI Bus, in its most recent service development planning study, identified corridors for limited-stop services connecting major suburban activity centers to the New York City subway network in Eastern Queens County. These corridors have significant travel in both directions; limited routes would supplement the local services, providing stops along the route at key activity nodes.

Performance Range

The performance range is derived from only two cases. In data from 1996, Route 134 provided 96 passenger trips per day, a rate of 5.3 passengers per trip. Route 133 performed better, with 115 passenger trips per day at a rate of 9.6 passengers per trip. Both services operate well below the system average of 20.73 passengers per trip for all suburban crosstown services, including locals and limiteds. However, ridership on both routes has nearly doubled over the past year, from 53 daily riders for Route 134 and 64 riders for Route 133. Both are still below expectations for this type of service, which were expected to approximate the system average for crosstown services of about 20 passengers per trip.

Conditions of Effectiveness

Limited services are designed to provide faster travel times for commuters than local bus services, thus making the transit option more attractive compared with the automobile during peak periods. Two planning factors appear important to the successful implementation of limited services:

- Presence of successful local service: Although only limited data are available from the case studies, it is apparent that limited services are more readily successful when they are used to upgrade existing services instead of to establish new services. DART is establishing a new service, and although it has the potential for long-term success, its slow growth pattern requires the patience to let the market build. Where a market is already established, limited services have the potential for built-in success with exiting riders, while choice riders are marketed and attracted to the new service.
- Concentrated stop activity and long trips: Limiteds stop only where there is significant activity. To have enough activity to justify the service, the corridor being served must have identifiable activity centers that will draw sufficient ridership; furthermore, passengers going to and from these centers need to come from far enough away so that the use of limited service is practical.

Implementing limited service is largely a technical exercise related to travel patterns, trip densities, and other operating factors. It is easiest to do in established local corridors, where load factors and travel times can readily establish the justification for the service. Planning is less clear when new services are being established and needs to be done slowly, with sufficient data, and in concert with the public/target market. In new markets, good data on origin-destination patterns, travel speeds, and complementing and competing services are essential when laying out new services, followed by marketing and development of public awareness. Planners must understand how the service will operate and what kinds of competitive advantages are offered over existing transit services and the single-occupant vehicle in order to accurately estimate the demand for the service. Focus groups and other outreach efforts taken in the planning phase of a project can help direct the planning effort toward services that reflect market desires.

CHAPTER 4

CIRCULATORS AND SHUTTLES

The second set of actions are those designed to complement the local bus network by featuring specialized services to smaller markets. Circulators are most often designed to supplement or perhaps substitute for line-haul services, where line-haul routes may be impractical because of street patterns, terrain, densities, or operating cost. Most offer local travel with connections to regional rail and bus services. Shuttles are developed to connect key activity centers and trip generators to the regional bus or rail network, providing the "missing link" in the regional network that might influence single-occupant vehicle users to try transit.

LOCAL AREA CIRCULATORS

Three generic types of local area circulators are identifiable from the case studies and are classified by their operating characteristics: fixed-route circulators (sometimes called service routes), route deviation services, and demand response or dial-a-ride services. Each is described separately below, although all three serve a common purpose: to improve mobility within and around a defined local area for internal trip making and for regional trips via transfers to the regional bus or rail network.

Examples of fixed-route suburban circulator services include:

- Perris/Route 30, Riverside Transit Agency ;
- Milwaukie Area, Tri-Met;
- Route 151/Sunnyside, Tri-Met;
- Willamette, Tri-Met;
- San Ramon Neighborhood Link, CCCTA;
- Route 103, CCCTA;
- Route 104, CCCTA;
- WhirleyBird, LANTA;
- Hackettstown Loop, NJ Transit; and
- Nassau Hub Shuttle.

Fixed-Route Suburban Circulator Services

The first category of circulators are those operated as fixed-route services.

Definition

Fixed-route circulators are differentiated from the regular local bus network by their configuration and purpose. The core routes of a suburban bus network are generally linear and are operated, for the most part, along arterial roadways. These routes are designed to offer direct, timely linkages between neighborhoods, communities, and multiple activity centers with a minimum of indirect segments into local communities. Circulator routes are designed to complement this network, offering services that penetrate into neighborhoods, provide localized trip making, and operate on secondary roadways. Circulator routes are generally confined to a single community, with intercommunity trips offered via transfers to other bus or rail services.

Circulator routes, by definition, circulate riders throughout a community. The routes are generally shorter than regular route services and are nonlinear, connecting multiple origins and destinations in the local area and penetrating into communities where regular fixed-route services cannot travel (Figure 30). Often, smaller buses or vans are used to provide this degree of penetration and accessibility. The trips made on circulators are short, and headways are generally short as well. With short headway and running times, these services are attractive alternatives to the short automobile trip with which they compete. In Madison, Wisconsin, Madison County, Illinois, and Toronto, circulator routes that are designed to meet the specialized needs of the elderly and disabled, but also provide service for the general public, are called service routes.

As complementary services, circulators support regional bus and rail networks and therefore are linked in at least one location for easy transfers to these services.

Applicability

Circulator services can offer an attractive option to the automobile for trips within a local community and can also help a regional transit operator maintain mobility within a service area where regular fixed routes would be prohibitive to provide. Based on the cases reviewed, the following conditions were identified for application of these services:

- In Hackettstown, New Jersey, the Hackettstown Loop was developed by NJ Transit to provide basic public transportation mobility in a community with no other local bus routes and only limited regional transit available.
- In Portland, three neighborhood services were developed by Tri-Met to circulate in areas where difficult

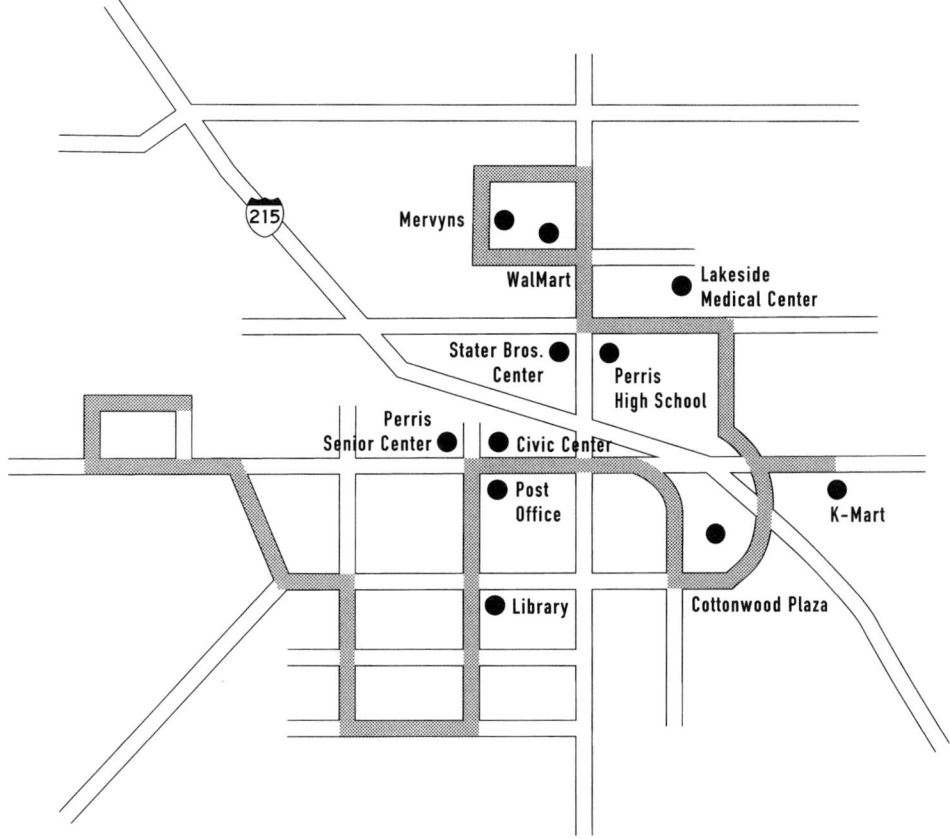

Figure 30. RTA Route 30, a suburban community circulator in Perris, Riverside County, California.

terrain, discontinuous roadways, and low-intensity development made it prohibitive to provide regular fixed-route services.
- In Walnut Creek, California, two CCCTA circulator routes were developed in and around the downtown area to link local activity centers and the BART station as a means of encouraging transit use and reducing secondary trip making, which was congesting downtown streets. The same objectives apply to the LI Bus Nassau Hub Shuttle on Long Island, which links major employment sites to a regional mall and other prime shopping locations.
- In Allentown, the LANTA WhirleyBird connects several shopping malls on a single route, allowing shoppers to park and ride between popular destinations. The route also connects to the regular route network at designated transfer centers (Figure 31).

There are a number of characteristics common to all applications. The routes were developed to conform to the desired lines of potential riders. Thus, the routes are rarely linear, use a combination of arterial and secondary roadways, and penetrate into neighborhoods, employment sites, and shopping centers to offer point-to-point service. These are routes that generally cannot be provided effectively as part of the regular, arterial-based local bus network and certainly not with full-sized equipment in most cases.

Besides providing local area service, each route connects to the regional bus or rail network in at least one location to provide feeder/distributor service for longer trip making. Two general types of services are provided—those designed to provide for multipurpose trips and general circulation, and those designed to meet very specific trip demands, in the cases cited, shopping trips.

Special purpose routes are almost uniformly short, with running times for one trip usually under 20 min. Passengers are generally expected to be on the buses for no longer than 10 min. Headways are frequent to ensure that the service is convenient to use, especially for midday trips among workers. Fares for these services are kept low to increase attractiveness and may be subsidized by employers. The general community circulators have fares similar to those on the regular route network operated by the regional provider, with free transfers provided between services. These routes tend to be longer and operate on more traditional headways, for example, 30-min peak services and 60- to 90-min off-peak services. The routes are generally longer, as they are usually the only routes in the community. The primary market for these routes are those individuals traditionally considered transit depen-

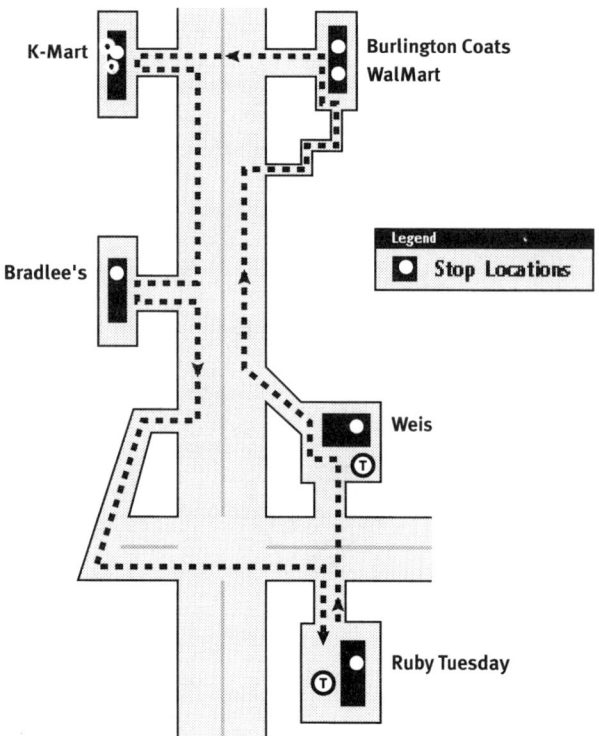

Figure 31. LANTA WhirleyBird Mall Express, Allentown, Pennsylvania.

dent who can accept the longer travel times and routings provided as a tradeoff for increased coverage.

Performance Range

The range of performance for fixed-route circulators is significant, from 22.0 trips per hour at the high end to 2.1 trips per hour at the low end (Table 5). However, in six of the nine cases cited, the range of performance was between 5 and 15 trips per hour, with a cluster around 8 to 10 trips per hour. A description follows.

There were two services among the case studies—the WhirleyBird in Allentown and Route 104 in Walnut Creek—with productivities well above those of the other services profiled.

LANTA, Allentown, Pennsylvania. The WhirleyBird Mall Express operates over a 10-hour period among five suburban shopping centers and is one of LANTA's most productive services. It operates every 30 min at a fare of $ 0.50; seniors ride free off-peak as part of a state subsidy program. WhirlyBird connects with other LANTA routes at two malls, and free transfers are provided. The malls' owners have been lukewarm to the service, allowing LANTA to post signs and have stops, but not helping to actively promote the service. Besides its productivity, a key to the WhirleyBird success is its labor arrangement with the LANTA operators union. The union has established a new wage rate of 60 percent of the standard wages and benefits for all new suburban shuttles; this allowed LANTA to keep the service in-house and created nine new positions for the union among all suburban services. It has also enabled LANTA to keep the cost per trip of its shuttles at reasonable levels compared with its traditional route network. One result is that LANTA uses a performance standard of 15.0 passengers per hour for its suburban services versus 29.0 for its urban routes. WhirleyBird easily exceeds this standard, in large part because of high senior ridership.

CCCTA, Walnut Creek, California. Routes 103 and 104 in Walnut Creek are operated by CCCTA (Figure 32) Route 103 is a new midday service sponsored jointly by the CCCTA and the city and operates on a figure-eight loop through the pedestrian-friendly suburban downtown area. Route 103 is called the "Free Ride" and operates from 9:00 AM to 4:00 PM

TABLE 5 Operating Performance of Fixed-Route Suburban Circulation Services

Subdistrict	Program	Passengers per Day	Passengers per Hour
Route 104 Walnut Creek	CCCTA	264	22.0
WhirleyBird Mall Express	LANTA	210	21.0
Milwaukie Area	Tri-Met	224	10-15 (est.)
Hackettstown Loop	NJ Transit	139	10.0 (est.)
Route 151/Sunnyside	Tri-Met	48	8-10 (est.)
Route 30/Perris	Riverside Transit		8.7
Willamette	Tri-Met	111	5-8 (est.)
Nassau Hub Shuttle	LI Bus		4.4 (new)
San Ramon Neighborhood Link	CCCTA		2.1

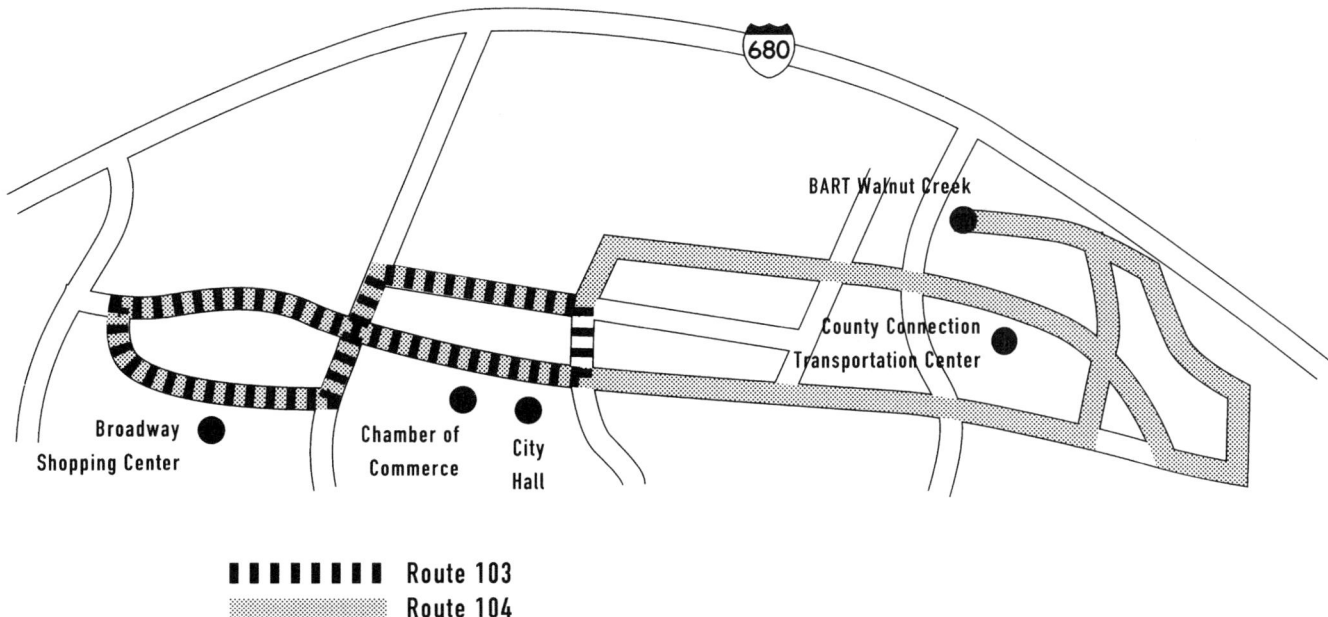

Figure 32. CCCTA Free Ride (Route 103) and Route 104, two fixed-route circulation services in Walnut Creek, California.

6 days a week on 5- to 7-min headway. It is considered highly successful, but no data were available on its performance. Route 104 is an established route that historically has operated within the downtown area on a similar loop route and that also links the downtown area to the local BART station, allowing it to serve commuters. Operated over a 12-hour period and coordinated with the BART schedule, this route provides a combination of local circulation, midlength commuter and multipurpose trips, and feeder/distribution services in a well-developed, dense Edge City environment. Given all these features, including strong local support and marketing, the service produces 22.0 passengers per hour at a cost of $1.11 per trip, both outstanding for the CCCTA program. The services meet the objectives of the program, to reduce secondary trip making, encourage transit use for commuter trips, and provide cost-effective mobility services to the community.

The San Ramon Neighborhood Link was the only very poorly performing service among the fixed-route circulators, with ridership at only 2.1 passengers per hour when it was discontinued. From 1992 to 1995, the CCCTA contracted for this service, which used two vans to circulate within two upper-middle income neighborhoods within the city of San Ramon. The service had 40-min headways and operated mainly on residential streets, with limited connections to an area shopping center. The lack of significant activity along the route, long headway for short trips, and income profile of the area were considered contributors to the performance of the service.

The remaining shuttles have productivities that range from 4.4 passengers per vehicle hour to approximately 15 passengers per vehicle hour, with a cluster of performance around 10 passengers per vehicle hour.

TRI-MET, Portland, Oregon. Tri-Met operates three neighborhood circulators, which began in the late 1980s. Originally, Tri-Met tried to implement general public demand response service in the Milwaukie area, but low ridership led to conversion first to route deviation and then, after enactment of the ADA, to fixed route. The Milwaukie circulator operates on a 30-min headway with a minibus, and averaged 224 passengers per day in September 1995. The Sunnyside area service was implemented based on the request of Clackamas County. The neighborhood is very hilly and has a discontinuous street network; analysis by Tri-Met indicated that regular fixed-route service would have difficulty penetrating the area and would probably have extremely low ridership. Two routes were implemented for Sunnyside—Route 151, a fixed-route circulator departing from the town center and looping through the highest density area of the community every 15 min during peak hours; and Route 150, a demand response service operated all day 6 days a week. The fixed-route portion of the service is geared to commuters meeting other Tri-Met services; in 1995, it provided approximately 48 trips per day or 8 to 10 trips per vehicle hour. The third Tri-Met shuttle operates in Willamette (Route 154), and was implemented based on requests from residents. The area is also hilly and difficult to serve with conventional buses. The circulator was designed as a loop through the residential neighborhoods, with connections provided to the Oregon City Transit Center. Peak half-hour and off-peak hour headways are provided. Ridership averaged 11 passengers per day in fall 1995, or about 5 to 8 passengers per vehicle hour.

The three Tri-Met services have daily ridership ranging from 48 passengers for the peak only Sunnyside service to

224 daily passengers for the Milwaukie service. Of the three, only the Milwaukie service is considered a moderate success; even so, the service does not attract a broad spectrum of users and relies heavily on a large senior population. One of the most significant problems with the service, however, is not productivity but operating cost. Once operated by contractors, the services are now operated by Tri-Met operators as a result of a dispute with their union.

NJ Transit, Hackettstown, New Jersey. The Hackettstown Loop operated by NJ Transit is another example of a circulator service designed as the primary bus service in a low-density suburban area. Hackettstown is an older, mature small city, once a center in rural northwestern New Jersey and now a city on the edge of growing suburban development. The loop is the first internal public transportation service operated there in many years and connects all of the city's principal neighborhoods and commercial activity centers. Being an older established community, the area is heavily automobile oriented, and the transit service has been slow to develop a core market. In fall 1995, ridership had reached 139 trips per day, and the cost recovery ratio, the key performance measure for NJ Transit, had reached 10.2 percent, still well below the agency goal of 25 percent after 2 years but double the rate since 1994.

Riverside Transit, Perris, California. The final fixed-route circulator from the case studies is Route 30 in Perris, in Riverside County. Perris is a rapidly suburbanizing older center, with new housing and malls being established around a low-density urban core (Figure 33). As the community develops, Riverside Transit is trying to meet localized needs with a circulator service linking new and developing areas. Using a contractor, the service operates on 30-min peak and 60-min off-peak headway. Ridership has doubled in the past year and is now at 8.4 passengers per hour. The cost recovery is still low, only 4 percent, and the subsidy per trip is still $4.50. Riverside Transit thinks the service is fulfilling its initial goals with respect to mobility issues and an overall policy aimed at providing transit options but has not yet established itself as an economically viable service.

Figure 33. Downtown Perris, Riverside County.

Conditions of Effectiveness

Based on the case studies described above and their range of performance, the following conditions have been identified, which appear to contribute to the strength and/or weakness of circulator services.

1. **Population and Population Density**—First and foremost, there must be enough people in the area to justify providing service. Second, the area should be reasonably dense for a fixed route to provide sufficient coverage and reasonable travel times. A compact operating environment favors bus service and enhances coverage.

2. **Transit Dependent Population**—Circulator services, designed for both captive and choice riders, need an established ridership base of transit-dependent individuals or a special circumstance that encourages people to leave the car behind. Seniors, moderate- and low-income riders, individuals with two wage earners but only one car represent the base market among many of these services. Commuters enhance the ridership potential where connections to regional rail and bus services are easy. Choice riders can be attracted to well-marketed and well-designed services, however, under special conditions. The Nassau Hub Shuttle (Figure 34) the two services in Walnut Creek operated by CCCTA, and the WhirleyBird are three examples of services with a mission to reduce secondary automobile travel in congested edge city or commercial corridor environments.

3. **Mixed-Use Setting or Special Conditions**—Besides having a sufficient population base from which to draw riders, successful routes have multiple, active local destinations. The greater the mix of uses, the better the opportunities are to link local trip origins and destinations with a logical circulator route and to sustain ridership over the entire day. Circulators geared to special uses—commuters, midday shoppers—may need to have schedules tailored to operate only during peak travel periods.

4. **Appropriate Headway and Travel Times**—To attract riders, the circulator services need to have attractive operating characteristics. The general purpose circulators, which provide basic transportation services within the community, have typical characteristics for local bus routes—headway at peak of 30 min and off peak of 60 to 90 min, 10 to 12 hours of service—and operate on routes suitable for covering the territory, which vary greatly in length. The primary market are the transit-dependent individuals in the community, augmented as much as possible by choice riders perhaps connecting to regional rail or bus in peak hours. The special shuttles, which rely to a large extent on choice riders and therefore must be attractive to them, generally have short

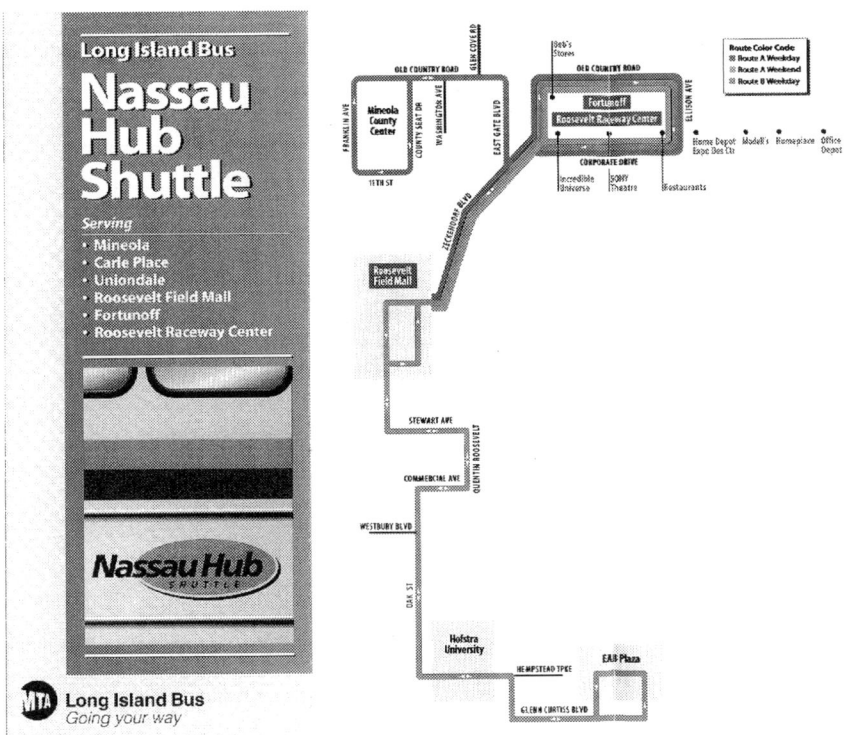

Figure 34. Nassau Hub Shuttle is a cooperative venture of LI Bus and local employers and businesses.

headways of 5 to 15 min and routes designed to capture short trips. Riders must perceive that the bus is more convenient to use than the car for a designated trip. Low fares, special equipment (Figure 35) attractive street furniture and waiting areas, and promotions all contribute to the success of these services.

5. **Low Operating Cost**—Fixed-route circulators often operate in environments where general fixed-route services cannot because of terrain, density, or street patterns. As a result, these routes generally have lower productivity than corresponding suburban routes. (This is not always the case—note that the Route 104 service, operating as a downtown circulator and as a shuttle to BART in Walnut Creek, is among the best routes for CCCTA.) Therefore, it is incumbent upon operators to keep costs down so that the cost per trip can be competitive with other services. Three methods were used in the case studies for controlling costs. Several operators contract for services with private operators. LANTA and LI Bus both negotiated separate wage rates for suburban drivers.

6. **Attractive Pricing**—General circulation services are usually priced in accordance with general transit fare policy as regular routes. A discount fare policy, however, is especially important for attracting choice riders to the special circulators. The CCCTA Walnut Creek circulator service is provided free, with the cost of the service borne by the local government and CCCTA. The Nassau Hub Shuttle fare is $ 0.25, whereas regular services are $1.50. The WhirleyBird costs $ 0.50 per trip but is free for seniors during off-peak hours.

7. **Coordinated Intermodal Connections**—All the circulators provide a connection to regional bus or rail services. By doing so, they enable riders to use the service not only for internal trip making but also for long-distance trips, including commuter trips during peak hours. Route 151 in Sunnyside, in fact, operates only

Figure 35. Route 104 shuttle bus at the Walnut Creek BART station.

at peak periods. Route 104 in Walnut Creek is one of CCCTA's best performing routes, largely because, in addition to local circulation, it provides a timed transfer to BART. The WhirleyBird connects in two locations with LANTA regular route buses and draws most of its riders from transfers.

Finally, strong local support in the planning process, coupled if possible with financial support for operations, and aggressive marketing are two cornerstones for all suburban transit activities.

Route Deviation Suburban Circulator Services

The second category of circulators are those operated as route deviation services. There were five of these services identified in the case studies, three in Broward County and two in Fort Worth. The three services in Broward County define themselves as fixed-route services, but a review of these programs indicates that each offers route deviation service, largely at the driver's discretion but well known to riders. The route deviation circulator services include:

- Margate, Broward County;
- Pembroke Pines, Broward County;
- Cooper City, Broward County;
- Richland Hills, Fort Worth; and
- Lake Worth, Fort Worth.

Definition

Circulators are differentiated from the regular local bus network by configuration and purpose, as previously described in the definition of fixed-route circulators. Circulators provide direct, timely linkages within communities, with connections to the regional rail or bus networks made available at designated transfer locations. The services themselves provide the primary public transportation resource within the community and as such complement the larger network with services that penetrate into neighborhoods that might otherwise be unserved.

Route deviation is used in each of the cases here to augment what are basically fixed-route circulator services. Each of the programs has a designated route and schedule, with specified stop locations and time points. Buses are allowed, however, to leave the route at any point to pick up riders in designated areas adjacent to the service as long as the buses then return to the route at the point of departure. There must be time in the schedule to allow for these deviations; this is a problem in some of the systems in Broward County, where the deviation service is less formally designated. Passengers using route deviation can board the buses at designated stops along the fixed route or can call a dispatcher to request a pickup off the route. Buses will also drop passengers off of the route; these requests are usually made directly to the driver.

With the potential for door-to-door service for any rider, route deviation provides an additional measure of convenience over fixed-route service while maintaining a fixed-route framework. Although this measure of convenience is at least in part aimed at attracting the choice rider, it clearly offers opportunities for door-to-door services for individuals needing special service who otherwise might require a demand response alternative and spreads the limited resources of the system to more areas of the community.

Thus, route deviation services are becoming increasingly important in meeting the requirements of the ADA within a cost-effective framework, because they do not require complementary paratransit services to be provided as for fixed routes.

Applicability

There were few examples of route deviation circulators among the 11 case studies. Those included are operated in moderately active areas, which are generally less dense than the areas served by fixed-route services. Route deviation services are used in these settings to expand coverage over the area without expending additional vehicle resources (vis-a-vis fixed route), offering a higher quality point-to-point service in the community. Route deviation is not used in areas of higher density where sufficient ridership can be generated from fixed-route services; thus, route deviation services generally have lower overall productivity than fixed-route service even with the added degree of convenience offered.

The routes themselves need to be developed to conform to the travel patterns of local residents and should connect origins and destinations logically using both arterial and secondary roadways. Although the routes may be circuitous, care should be taken to maintain reasonable travel times that do not excessively delay riders. Appropriate equipment should be used, reflecting the operating environment; in most cases this would be a small bus or van.

There are a number of specific concerns with implementing route deviation:

- The number of deviations on any single trip needs to be monitored to ensure that the overall operating schedule can be maintained and that riders are not experiencing excessive delays in making their trips.
- The operating environment needs to be conducive to route deviation. Buses need to be able to exit and enter the route easily to avoid excess operating delays. Thus, care and attention must be paid to the road network and traffic patterns and congestion when considering route deviation.
- Route deviation services must be monitored with regard to the location of boardings and alightings. As common

patterns emerge, it is possible that repeating patterns of deviations might lend themselves to a route change.
- Route deviation services are not readily applicable in situations that are highly time sensitive unless measures are taken to ensure a high degree of travel time reliability.

Performance Range

The performance range for route deviation generally falls between fixed-route and demand response services (Table 6), with the operating environment, land-use density, and quality of the service being factors influencing ridership.

As noted in the conditions for applicability, route deviation services are generally not implemented in densely populated, high-activity centers. For example, circulators in edge cities are provided by fixed-route services. The five applications cited here are all route deviation services operated in moderate density environments. The three in Broward County are operated in mixed-use communities, and the two in Fort Worth are operated in residential neighborhoods.

The three community circulators in Broward County were implemented as part of a county policy aimed at maintaining neighborhood mobility while divesting the county system of unproductive services and route segments. Broward County policy is to develop interlocal agreements with interested suburban municipalities, under which they can lease small vehicles at nominal rates and receive annual operating funds of $18,000 per vehicle per year. The services that are then provided are designed and operated by the local municipality. The program design allows for a more personalized, demand-driven transit service within the local jurisdiction, with connections to the county bus system operated along principal arterials and providing regional connections.

Each of the communities operates fixed-route services that allow for route deviation requests. The local circulators were developed to provide internal circulation and maintain local mobility in light of possible service costs by Broward County. They replaced the service the regional bus network could not provide efficiently within the context of its overall local bus structure. Margate, with a population of 42,985 and a density of 5,320 persons per mi^2 (2.6 km^2), offers the most extensive program, with four routes serving the community. Cooper City has a population of only 20,791 persons and a density of 4,154 persons and provides one route. Pembroke Pines, which has the largest population (85,947), has the lowest density of the three communities (2,691 persons per mi^2) and also provides one route. Margate has the oldest population of the three (30.4 percent over 65 years of age), highest rate of mobility-limited persons between 16 and 64 years of age (7 percent), and lowest median household income ($28,465). Development in Margate is older than in the other two communities. Pembroke Pines is the least dense community. Only 19.4 percent of the population is over 65 year of age, and the household income is $36,431. Development is relatively new and continuing in this balanced, mixed-use suburb. Cooper City is the smallest of the three communities, covering only 6.3 mi^2 (16.3 km^2), and has the youngest population, with only 7.0 of the residents over 65 years of age. The median household income is $49,750, well above the other communities and the county average. Development is very new and characterized by largely single-family residential developments and clustered, small shopping centers along principal arterials. It is the most residential of the three settings.

As noted, the Margate service is the most dense, with four routes operated 6 days a week, with four weekday routes and three Saturday routes. A single expanded route provides holiday service. Three routes have operated since 1993, and the fourth was added in late 1995. Service is provided to over 70 percent of the community. Service connects to the Broward County system at three locations. Cooper City's route has operated since 1991 on Monday through Saturday. The service was specifically implemented in response to plans to discontinue county service in the community. The circulator is designed to connect residents of this largely residential community to the civic center and one county bus route, which are outside walking distance for most people. Finally, Pembroke Pines operates a single route, which connects residents, the hospital, a mall, and the community center, and which provides connections to two county bus routes.

The three programs are operated by city departments. Pembroke Pines operates the service through Community Services, with the Senior Center Transportation Administrator managing it as well as senior transportation services.

TABLE 6 Operating Performance of Route Deviation Suburban Circulation Services

Service	Program	Passengers per Hour	Cost per Passenger
Margate	Broward County	11.6	$ 1.86
Cooper City	Broward County	9.6	2.74
Richland Hills	Fort Worth	8.1	5.13
Pembroke Pines	Broward County	6.4	3.43
Lake Worth	Fort Worth	4.3	10.29

Service is provided over approximately 11 hours on 90-min headways. Cooper City runs its services through the Senior Service Program as well and uses a combination of paid and volunteer staff. The route operates approximately 10 hours a day on 90-min headways. The city of Margate service is provided through the Department of Public Works and is staffed by a transit coordinator responsible for operations. Its four routes provide the most dense coverage among the three programs as well as the least flexibility with regard to route deviations. Service is provided over a 12-hour period on 60-min headways.

The performance characteristics among the three services vary, from a high of 11.6 passengers per vehicle hour in Margate to a low of 6.4 passengers per vehicle hour in Pembroke Pines. Cooper City has a productivity of 9.6 passengers per vehicle hour. In comparison, the average productivity of the Broward County network is 31.63 passengers per vehicle hour; therefore, the best of the three routes operates at about one-third of the county average. What really distinguishes these services, and makes them successful in the eyes of the county and local communities, is the cost per passenger trip rates of the three, which vary from $1.86 in Margate to $3.43 in Pembroke Pines. Cooper City is at $2.74. The county program operates at a rate of $1.86 per passenger trip. Thus, because of the very attractive cost structures of the community-based systems, which range from about $22.00 to $25.00 per hour in compared with $55.77 for the county system, these services meet overall cost-effectiveness criteria for the program. As an additional benefit, the ridership and productivity of the county bus system has improved since the start of these programs, as routes were restructured to eliminate nonproductive segments and improve directness and running times on arterial roadways.

With regard to the variation in performance among the three systems, it is apparent that the density of the network in Margate, coupled with its favorable population profile, account for its position as the best of the three.

With regard to service density, Margate provides 2.5 service mi (4.02 km) per capita, versus 1.1 mi (1.77 km) for Cooper City and 0.60 mi (0.97 km) for Pembroke Pines. Similarly, it provides 0.17 hour of service per capita versus 0.05 for Cooper City and 0.04 for Pembroke Pines. This higher level of service translates into more coverage, better headways, and a more useful service to the community.

Cooper City and Pembroke Pines both operate one route with similar levels of service, yet Cooper City operates at about 150 percent of the productivity and cost-effectiveness of Pembroke Pines, despite having one-third of the population. One of the major issues in both locations, but felt more strongly in Pembroke Pines, is how to serve the community with a single vehicle, (e.g., how to trade off coverage and level of service). The routes in both places have been continuously stretched and route deviation used to extend service to as much of the community as possible. The result has been problematic—more coverage has been provided but often at the expense of on-time performance and reliability. Regular users love the flexibility and convenience of the systems, but the service quality is reaching the point where the viability of the program may become threatened. As trip lengths are extended and routes made increasingly indirect, the services become less attractive to all but a core of transit-dependent persons. The problem is more acute in Pembroke Pines, which has an area of 31.9 mi^2 (82.62 km^2) (though much of it is in the undeveloped Everglades), than in Cooper City, a relatively compact area of 6.3 mi^2 (16.32 km^2).

Whereas the three services in Broward County are designated as fixed-route programs offering route deviation services, the two in Fort Worth were specifically designed and marketed as route deviation programs. In 1995, based on a review of six key performance indicators of productivity and cost-effectiveness, the Fort Worth Transportation Authority (The T) began to develop a series of innovative transportation services to replace marginal fixed routes with specialized suburban services. Using small vehicles and flexible routes, The T initiated the Richland Hills Rider Request and the Lake Worth DoorStep Direct (Figures 36 and 37).

Richland Hills is a compact community with a high proportion of retired residents who typically have destinations within the city limits. To address these transportation needs more efficiently, planners modified service on an existing bus route to provide route deviation within Richland Hills. Passengers have the option of calling The T to schedule a pickup one day in advance or calling the bus driver directly for same day pickup. Vehicles are scheduled to leave downtown Fort Worth every 90 min between 6:15 AM and 6:15 PM on weekdays only. Once the vans reach Richland Hills, they drop off and pick up passengers within the community for 45 min and then return to downtown Forth Worth. The T uses 10-passenger vans; drivers are equipped with a cellular telephone. One-way fares are 80 cents; students, seniors, and disabled patrons pay 40 cents.

Lake Worth is a residential area with peak-period commuters destined for downtown Fort Worth and an all-day demand for the Southside Medical District outside downtown. To respond more efficiently to these demands, planners scheduled fixed-route service with limited route deviation. The fixed-route service combined service to downtown Fort Worth with a loop that circulated within Lake Worth. The Fort Worth T replaced the fixed-route local circulator with a 20-min demand responsive segment on the outbound trip from downtown. Passengers may reserve a pickup time at their homes during this time. Passengers must make reservations 24 hours in advance; fares are comparable with the rest of the system. The route uses 26-ft (7.92 m) 18-passenger minibuses. Although The T lost passengers at first, ridership eventually increased by about 10 percent.

Rider Request and DoorStep Direct are both slightly more expensive to operate than the system's fixed routes. The cost per hour of the services are $43.89 and $41.40, respectively, versus $39.18 for the system as a whole. On a per mile basis,

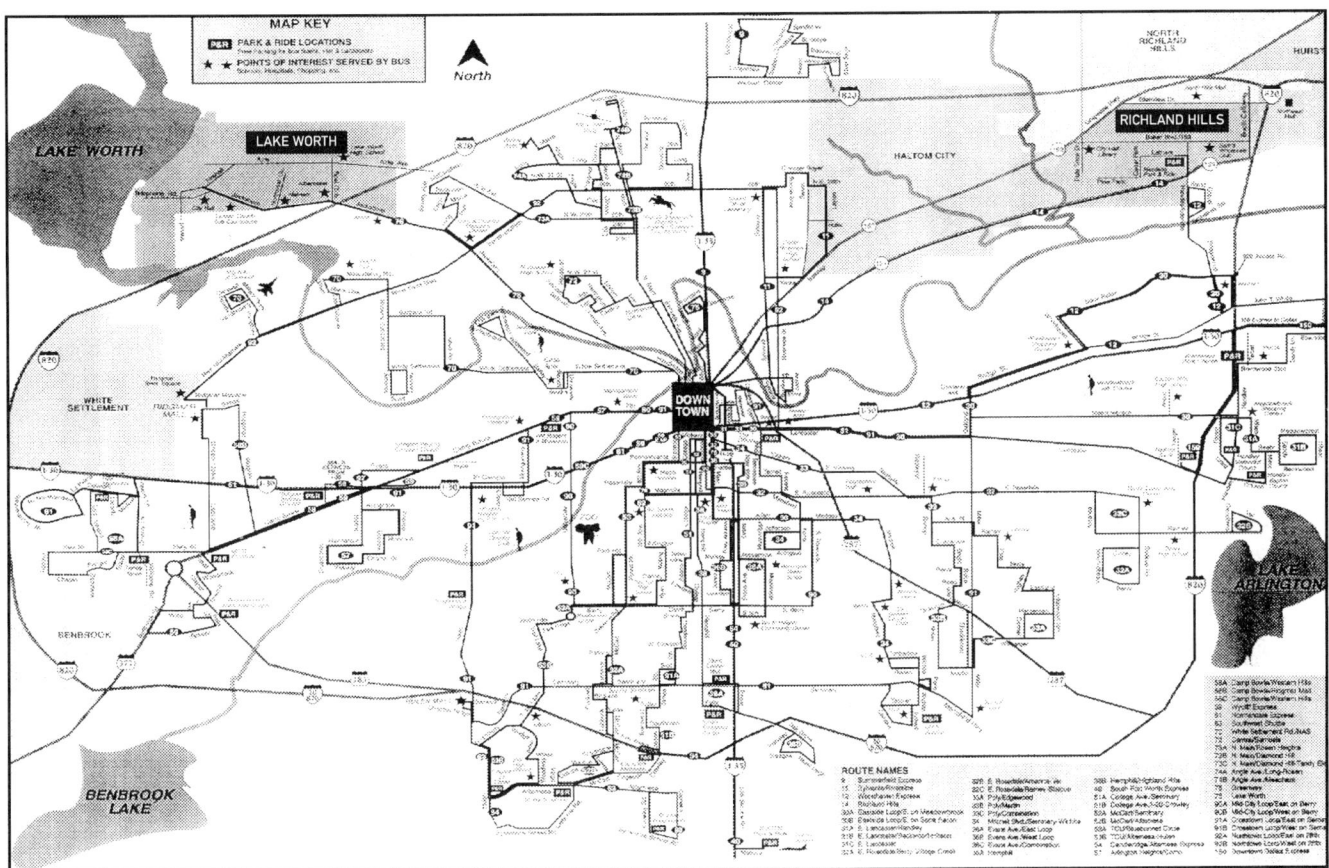

Figure 36. Fort Worth Transit Network showing the route deviation service zones in Lake Worth and Richland Hills.

they are actually less expensive to operate; achieving higher operating speeds than the system average, they operate at $2.50 and $2.62, respectively versus $2.74 for the system. Although the passenger per hour rates are only a fraction of the system average, at 4.26 in Richland Hills and 8.07 in Lake Worth versus 17.35 systemwide, these rates are higher than those for the fixed-service segments they replaced. Thus,

Figure 37. Special vehicles used by "The Ride" in Fort Worth for its route deviation services.

although the cost per passenger trip is $10.29 for the Richland Hills service and $5.13 for the Lake Worth service, the costs are actually lower than the cost per trip for the previous service. Given the goal of maintaining suburban mobility to these neighborhoods, the changes have actually achieved a net savings for The T. The disparity in performance between the two systems appears to be a function of the community profile and their desired trip-making activities. Lake Worth has a larger percentage of peak-period commuters destined for downtown Fort Worth, as well as an all-day demand for service to a medical district located outside the CBD. Richland Hills, on the other hand, has a higher proportion of retired residents who typically make shorter, intracommunity trips.

The range of productivity for route deviation circulator services is from 4.3 to 11.6 passengers per vehicle hour. In Broward County, where the operating costs are low, the cost per trip ranges from $1.86 to $3.43; in Fort Worth, which is not contracted, the higher cost of the operation results in a cost per trip of $5.13 to $10.29. Regardless of the outcome, even the high-end costs are meeting system objectives in both areas, as mobility continues to be provided in areas where regular services have previously failed. Judging from the performance of these services, productivities for these services in ideal conditions should range between 10 and 15 passengers per hour; if costs are kept low, the cost per trip of the most efficient services should be comparable to the cost per trip of the regular fixed-route network.

Conditions of Effectiveness

What are the conditions of effectiveness that contribute to the success and/or failure of these services to meet expected performance levels?

1. **Population and Population Density**—Although there must be enough persons to justify providing services, the total population, and particularly the population density, should be more moderate than for fixed routes so that total demand and demand for route deviations does not exceed the capacity of the program. A compact operating environment will enhance the service, as evidenced in Cooper City compared with the same type of program in Pembroke Pines.
2. **Continuous Roadways**—To provide route deviations, the bus must be able to leave and return to the route efficiently in order to minimize excess running time.
3. **Transit-Dependent Profile**—Four of the five services rely to a great extent on nonchoice riders, particularly the elderly. The fifth, the Lake Worth DoorStep Direct, has a significant choice rider group among commuters, who are able to make a one-seat trip from their doorstep to downtown Fort Worth. This service, along with the WhirleyBird, Route 104 in Walnut Creek and the Nassau Hub Shuttle, demonstrates that services can be designed and marketed to choice riders in selected venues if conditions are right and the services are comfortable, convenient, and well-marketed.
4. **Mixed-Use Setting**—The more productive services were those operated with appropriate levels of service in mixed-use settings, serving a mixture of residential and commercial and civic activities.
5. **Appropriate Level of Service**—Even if all other conditions are right—density, mix of activities, street network, marketing—it is essential to provide an appropriately designed service. The basic routes need to connect origins and destinations in a reasonably direct manner, allowing for some deviation and circuity, and headways need to be accommodating. Clearly, one of the problems associated with the Pembroke Pines service is its inability to serve 31.6 mi^2 (81.8 km^2) with a single route; deviations and route modifications have created a route with an 80-min running time and 90-min headways, which limits the effectiveness of the service and its value to all but a core of transit dependents. Cooper City also operates on long headways, but the running time of each loop is only 38 min. In Richland Hills, the Lake Worth service operates for 20 min in its route deviation segment and and then goes direct to downtown Fort Worth. The one-seat service for trips within the community or to the CBD is a very attractive feature and one that contributes to the high choice ridership of the service.
6. **Low Operating Cost**—Once again, it is important to note that the competitive operating costs of these programs can play a significant role in determining cost-effectiveness and goal attainment. The Broward County services have cost structures that are a fraction of the County structure and thus are successful programs on a cost per trip basis despite productivity levels of one-third or less than the County network. In Fort Worth, the service is operated by The T so that there is no cost advantage; the cost-effectiveness of this program is achieved because the new services are attracting more riders than those they replaced, thus preserving suburban mobility.
7. **Coordinated Intermodal Connections**—Intermodal connections are a major attraction for these services, which serve as feeders and distributors for the regional network. In Fort Worth, the services are designed to eliminate the transfer entirely; in Broward County, transfers are designated at a number of terminals in each community.
8. **Local Support and Public Participation**—The Fort Worth Transportation Authority credits its extensive public outreach program with identifying innovative service needs. In addition to working with local residents and elected officials with regard to proposed service changes, the authority has a 24-hour telephone line for residents to record their comments. The Broward County services were designed locally, with the inputs of citizens, elected officials, and city staff. The program is the community's program in each case, designed by themselves for their needs and funded by the taxpayers. One of the hallmarks of these programs, according to riders, is their friendliness and willingness to go out of the way for their customers.
9. **Marketing**—The Forth Worth T promoted services in Lake Worth and Richland Hills through direct marketing. For example, residents in Richland Hills received an information packet describing Rider Request service as well as a refrigerator magnet listing the reservation telephone number.

Demand Response Suburban Circulator Services

The final set of suburban circulators are those that are operated as demand response, door-to-door programs. Often called dial-a-ride services, the case studies and research identified nine applications among five operators. Examples of this type of service include:

- El Cajon, San Diego Transit;
- Spring Valley, San Diego Transit;

- La Mesa, San Diego Transit;
- Maxi-Ride, Tidewater Transit District;
- Sunnyside, Tri-Met;
- DARTAbout, DART;
- Mays Landing, NJ Transit;
- Northfield, NJ Transit; and
- Absecon, NJ Transit.

Definition

Demand response or dial-a-ride services are used as circulators in a number of settings. These systems provide door-to-door dropoff and pickup within a designated service area, are available to the general public, and generally operate throughout the day. Advance notice for trip reservations varies among services, from 1 hour to 1 day in advance of a trip; standing orders are accepted for trips. Most of the services have reciprocal transfer arrangements with the regional network; in some cases transfers are free and in others there is a small transfer charge.

Applicability

Demand response services are generally applied in areas of low to moderate density where the number of transit trips and size of the area would probably be insufficient to justify a network of fixed-route services. Demand response services are intended to provide greater area coverage with fewer vehicle resources than a fixed-route network. At the same time, by offering a door-to-door premium service, they provide an additional level of service that planners and operators hope to translate into higher ridership among choice riders.

Dial-a-ride services in San Diego, for example, were initiated to overcome problems of dispersed trip making and low-density suburban development patterns, along with a development pattern of cul-de-sacs and discontinuous streets that limit traffic and opportunities for fixed-route transit. In many areas, these problems are exacerbated by the local topography, with hills and canyons that inhibit direct connections between neighboring communities, restrict the use of the roads to small vehicles, and make pedestrian access to bus stops virtually impossible.

Dial-a-ride services were specifically developed to overcome these barriers to conventional bus services, providing mobility to areas that otherwise would be unserved and feeder services to the regional rail and bus network.

General public demand response service has a history of unsuccessful ventures, of the nine programs identified in the research, four have been discontinued because of lack of ridership support and escalating costs. Another service identified in the case studies, operated by LANTA and designated as a general public dial-a-ride, is, for all intents and purposes, a specialized service for seniors, because the 3-day

Figure 38. San Diego Transit's La Mesa transfer center.

advance notice policy for reservations effectively eliminates the service's utility for those with the option of driving.

Where general public dial-a-ride has worked best is where it has functioned not only as a general circulator but also as a shuttle to mainline rail and bus services. San Diego has two sets of dial-a-ride services—the community circulator programs in El Cajon, Spring Valley, and La Mesa, and the DART (Direct Access to Regional Transit Services) shuttle program in six locations, which is described in the section on shuttles (Figure 38). Tidewater Regional Transit operates a successful program, Maxi-Ride, which combines general community circulation with feeder service to the mainline bus system (Figure 39). Finally, the Sunnyside Dial-a-Ride in Portland, despite having somewhat disappointing ridership as of 1995, continues to operate in conjunction with a peak-hour fixed-route circulator.

To succeed, dial-a-ride programs need to be focused, with tightly defined territories and rules that help create cost-effective runs. This is the case for the systems in Tidewater, San Diego, and Portland and is underscored by experiences in Hamilton, Ohio, and Orange County, California, with dial-a-rides. Hamilton replaced many of its local fixed routes

Figure 39. A Tidewater regional transit Maxi-Ride vehicle waits at a suburban transit center along with buses from the fixed-route network.

with minibuses and vans that circulate within designated wedges of the city; travel between wedges is made on mainline transit routes and from a downtown transfer center. Orange County has created a similarly zoned network of dial-a-ride services; vehicles stay within their designated zones, and interzone trips are made by transferring between vehicles for parties of fewer than five passengers. Orange County uses advanced automated technologies to increase operating efficiencies; these advances ultimately may help dial-a-ride programs create cost-efficient services. Improved scheduling and dispatching, automated real time vehicle location technology, electronic mapping, and cellular communications technologies are increasingly being tested to create "smart" forms of dial-a-ride, which can be more responsive to traveler needs and more effective in creating efficient vehicle runs that ultimately will drive up productivity and bring down the cost per trip of these services.

Performance Range

Of the nine services identified, four have been terminated because of poor operating performance. Because the two operators, NJ Transit and DART, kept ridership data and cost data differently, direct performance comparisons are difficult to make, not only between these services, but between these services and those still in operation.

In Dallas, DARTAbout was initiated in 1989 after a series of service cuts in the fixed-route network. Service coverage was limited to a few suburban communities and to areas beyond the coverage of the fixed-route network. These services were intended to provide local circulation and feeder services, but only 23 percent of the riders reported transferring to other services. Most of the riders were regular, core users—83 percent of the trips were subscription trips, and 44 percent of the passengers reported using the service 5 days or more per week. The ridership base never increased significantly, and the service was discontinued in 1995. Average daily ridership at that time was 286 passenger trips; average Saturday ridership was 53 trips. When the service was discontinued, the cost was about $12.40 per passenger trip versus a system average of $2.50 per passenger trip.

The three NJ Transit services were implemented as part of an experimental program testing various types of suburban delivery services around the state. The three services were all in Atlantic County and were designed to connect low-density residential communities to a midsized regional employment corridor. The service was initiated by NJ Transit working with Atlantic County planning staff and had minimal support from the employers themselves. Furthermore, this was not a service the community at large asked for or initiated, so there was a low level of public support and awareness of the project. Coupled with the relatively short travel distances and minor roadway congestion and parking issues, the project was unable to generate significant ridership from any of the three areas. The range of ridership reported by NJ Transit was from 8 to 15 passenger trips per day, or less than 2 trips on average for any run to or from the employment sites. The cost recovery ratio, which was the basis for determining goal attainment for the experimental program, ranged from 4 to 10 percent after 2 years, well below the 25 percent standard for maintaining a service.

The five programs that continue to operate are all based in areas that are well-defined, have a number of activity centers, and have a moderate population base in terms of both size and density. Three are located in San Diego, and there is one each in Tidewater and Portland.

No area of the country has accumulated a longer history of experience with general public DAR services than metropolitan San Diego. In 1974, officials from El Cajon, a suburb 15 mi (24.1 km) east of downtown San Diego, contracted with San Diego Yellow Cabs, Inc., to provide a "turnkey" DAR service, called the El Cajon Express. As designed, the El Cajon Express operated 7 days a week, 24 hours a day anywhere within the city; for trips to destinations outside of El Cajon, vehicles operated like exclusive-ride, metered taxis. Reservations could be made with only 1 hour notice required. By 1980, ridership on the El Cajon Express grew to around 600 trips per day, and at a dollar fare per trip the service covered around 30 percent of its costs, comparable to fixed-route bus services in the area. The same year, the El Cajon Express was averaging around 8 passengers per vehicle hour, a decent rate of productivity for a community-based service. Other suburban communities in greater San Diego, including La Mesa and Spring Valley, followed suit, contracting their own general public DAR services.

As San Diego's trolley line extended into the eastern suburbs in the mid-1980s (Figure 40), thus providing another mobility option for the region, and the cost of curb-to-curb contract services continually increased, the financial performance of general public DAR services began to falter. Ridership levels have fallen off in El Cajon to fewer than 100 passenger trips per day [21,612 passenger trips for fiscal year (FY) 1995], and

Figure 40. El Cajon Station intermodal transfer point between the San Diego Trolley and local buses and paratransit.

the cost of operations has dramatically increased, to $3.33 per mi. The La Mesa service carried 59,236 passengers in FY 1995, about triple that of El Cajon, and Spring Valley carried a similar number of trips, 19,199, in FY 1995. The respective operating costs for the two services were $2.52 per mi in La Mesa and $3.02 in Spring Valley.

These cost per mile figures, although growing, are still low compared with the cost of the local fixed-route services provided by San Diego Transit, which were $3.99 in FY 1995. However, even with the cost differential obtained from private contracts, the subsidy per passenger and cost recovery ratios are very low compared with the fixed-route service because the productivity of the services is very low compared with local fixed routes.

Productivity for SDT local fixed routes in FY 1995 was 2.53 passengers per mi, versus 0.33 for La Mesa, 0.25 for El Cajon, and 0.30 for Spring Valley. As a result, per rider deficits on San Diego's DAR services, which were $2 to $3 in 1988–1990, are now $6.25 to $11.50, compared with $0.84 for a local fixed-route bus. The fare recovery ratios range from 12.5 percent in Spring Valley to 18.0 percent in La Mesa and are 46.5 percent for the fixed-route services. Premium fares for the door-to-door service compared with fixed-route fares help keep the cost recovery levels at these rates—Spring Valley charges $1.50 per trip and $0.50 with a transfer, whereas El Cajon charges $4.00 per trip but $2.00 for seniors and the disabled and $0.50 with a transfer.

These data do not demonstrate that fixed-route service would operate more effectively or efficiently in these communities. As discussed earlier, the experiences in Broward County and Fort Worth indicate that fixed-route services in low to moderate density environments often are less productive than the services that replace them, even when the services have low productivity rates, because of the inability of fixed routes to provide sufficient coverage, difficult terrain, or transit-unfriendly development patterns. On the other hand, in Broward County and Fort Worth, the operating and financial data suggested that the replacement services were, on a cost-per-trip basis, reasonably similar to the fixed-route programs, which is not the case in San Diego. Currently, both El Cajon and La Mesa are considering replacing general public DAR with fixed-route shuttle vans that feed into trolley stations.

Tidewater Transit's Maxi-Ride is the most successful example of regional DAR services open to the general public. Maxi-Ride operates mainly in low-density areas of Norfolk-Chesapeake-Portsmouth. Each vehicle is equipped with a cellular phone. Passengers request rides by calling drivers directly. This eliminates the cost of a central dispatcher. Drivers log in service requests, schedule pickups and dropoffs, and determine routing. This makes for a very efficient, cost-controlled service.

From 6 AM to 7 PM, Monday through Saturday, each of six Maxi-Ride zones is served by a free-roaming minibus that ties into a direct transfer center at regular intervals. Someone wishing a ride can board at a transfer center within the zone or can call 2 hours in advance for front-door service. Riders can travel anywhere within the service area on a single Maxi-Ride vehicle. To leave the service zone, however, they must transfer to a fixed-route bus at a transfer center or to a Maxi-Ride service in an adjacent territory. All transfers are synchronized to the maximum extent possible through driver-to-driver cellular phone communications. TRT provides a variety of fare options for the general public to patronize Maxi-Ride, including one-zone monthly Fare Cutter Cards of $20 plus $1.35 per trip and All-Zone Cards (good for traversing any of the 10 zones) for $38 plus $0.80 per trip.

For the three lowest density Maxi-Ride zones, the average operating subsidy per passenger was $2.17 to $4.67 in fall 1995. TRT's subsidy per passenger for fixed-route services ranges from a modest profit to $7.04; the average per passenger fixed-route subsidy is $0.94. Thus, in light of the excellent quality of service provided, Maxi-Ride is viewed locally as an unqualified success, providing services in low-density areas where fixed-route costs would be excessive at a cost per trip, which is reasonable given the range experienced for fixed-route services.

Originally, the cost-effectiveness was achieved by maintaining low operating costs through competitively contracting the service to a private taxi company. However, during 1983–1986 contract negotiations, TRT's labor representatives agreed to create a minibus paratransit division whose drivers would receive reduced salaries and operate under few work rule restrictions. This resulted in TRT eventually winning the Maxi-Ride service in the mid-1980s and operating it entirely in-house, a pattern earlier identified for suburban initiatives at LANTA and LI Bus.

The Sunnyside dial-a-ride in Portland, identified as Tri-Met Route 150, operates all day from Monday through Saturday and is supplemented by Route 151, a peak-hour circulator service. The service provides connections at the town center to regional transit and circulates to almost all areas of this mixed-use community. It was implemented to provide mobility over a hilly terrain, which was unsuitable for fixed-route services with full-sized transit coaches. Tri-Met originally used contractors for this and other community services, but a dispute with the driver's union led to the program being operated in-house as of 1993, which increased the cost by about 100 percent. As of summer 1995, ridership was 114 passengers per day, which was below anticipated levels, and efforts were undertaken to modify the service area.

With the exception of Maxi-Ride, dial-a-ride services not meeting expectations among all the operators with regard to the number of trips provided or the productivity and cost-effectiveness of the programs. Ridership levels in most systems seldom exceed a few passengers per vehicle hour, and subsidy per trip levels and cost recovery rates are poor, even where services are contracted. Subsidy per trip rates in Dallas and San Diego, which were reported, far exceed the rates for the local fixed-route services; cost recovery rates ranged from as low as 4 percent in Mays Landing, New Jersey, to 18 percent in La Mesa. Maxi-Ride stands out among the case studies; as such, some of the lessons learned are incorporated into the following discussion.

Conditions of Effectiveness

As described, dial-a-ride programs for the general public have only a modest success rate in suburban areas. Although technological changes are constantly improving the responsiveness of these services, which may translate into better and more effective programs, some basic issues must be addressed when these programs are developed, many of which are interrelated.

1. **Appropriate Setting**—Dial-a-ride services work best in low to moderate density settings, which are too sparsely population or lack the density for fixed-route service. Many of the territories also feature terrain that is unnavigable by full-sized coaches or street patterns on which coaches are unable to travel. In these settings, dial-a-ride programs penetrate neighborhoods, provide greater areawide coverage, and feed fixed-route services at transit centers or along major arterial roadways.
2. **Focused, Well-Defined Service Area**—Part and parcel of the above factor is the need to carefully define and bound the service area. Successful services constrain coverage either in this manner or by restricting the way trips are provided (see below). Given that the appropriate setting may be large with low density, extending coverage too far with inadequate resources will negatively affect productivity and cost-effectiveness, as trip lengths are extended and opportunities for trip-grouping are reduced.
3. **Limiting Trips**—The more successful examples of dial-a-ride programs have limited trip making, especially between designated zones, which concentrates activity and enables operators to maximize the use of resources. Interzone trips are made via connection to fixed-route services at designated transfer points. Within a zone, operators still allow for all origin-destination pairs, which provide the circulator function within the community for which the program was designed.
4. **Intermodal Opportunities**—In conjunction with the limitation on trip patterns, successful programs need to focus on two patterns: internal trip making within a zone/community, and external trip making between communities. With respect to the latter, a key focal point of successful programs is an intermodal terminal—for example, in San Diego it is the trolley station and in Tidewater it is designated suburban bus terminals. Circulators then provide two functions, local circulation and feeder/distribution for the regional network, thus increasing utility. Furthermore, the regional trip patterns attract choice users more than the local trip opportunities, further enhancing the potential of the service.
5. **Transit-Dependent Population**—Local circulation trip making for the most part serves the transit dependent (Figure 41). As these are generally short trips, choice riders generally will use their cars for these trips, unless there is a prevailing local issue restricting the convenience of the automobile—congestion around activity centers, parking congestion or pricing, and so forth. Therefore, the service area should have a reasonably high number of transit dependents—older individuals, low or moderate income families, one car households, teenagers—to ensure the presence of a base rider population.
6. **Use of New Technologies for Real-Time Scheduling**—Perhaps the most critical factor that will contribute to the success of existing and planned demand response services will be the introduction of new technologies to these programs. As hardware becomes less costly, operators will be able to use new scheduling and dispatching programs that feature automatic vehicle location (AVL) detection, geographic information systems (GIS), and cellular communications technologies, which will translate into better, quicker responses to travel requests. Tidewater already has shifted to immediate response by placing cellular phones on each vehicle and allowing drivers to set schedules, which makes the Maxi-Ride as easy to use as the fixed-route bus. Systems will be able to overcome response-time issues, and use the AVL and GIS programs to track vehicles and improve on-time performance and reliability.
7. **Reasonable Operating Costs**—This topic has been covered previously in these guidelines and is one of the foundations for success in suburban mobility. Tidewater operates its services by using a reduced labor rate negotiated with its operators union, and the San Diego services are contracted to private operators. Only Tri-

Figure 41. A TRT Maxi-Ride van drops off a worker at a Burger King in suburban Norfolk.

Met operates its own service and does so only because of a dispute with their operators union.

8. **Modest Goals and Objectives Focused on Mobility and Cost-Effectiveness**—Even after taking all the above factors into account, a fundamental tenet to suburban mobility planning, particularly with demand response services with their lower ridership counts, is to focus on realistic goals and objectives and to remember those when evaluating operations. The focal point for assessing the projects must be on cost-effectiveness, the cost per trip of these services, and not on productivity or sheer volume, neither of which will approach the levels of fixed-route operations. Are these services providing trips at reasonable cost compared with the fixed-route program? Was the cost per trip better when fixed-route services were provided or, if they were, could fixed-route service do better? Even more important, if maintaining regional mobility is an objective for the area, is the cost of the service reasonable to maintain regional mobility in areas where fixed-route service cannot operate effectively? Assessing the total ridership or productivity of demand response and fixed-route services is comparing apples and oranges—the very different environments make such comparisons meaningless. Mobility and cost-effectiveness, on the other hand, can be measured and compared more readily and are a more logical foundation upon which to assess success or failure.

SHUTTLE SERVICES

Shuttle services are used to supplement the existing transit network by providing tailored, high-quality connecting services between major activity centers, one of which is often a transit center. Their purpose is to make regional rail or bus travel a more viable option for travelers by creating the final link in the public transportation network—the home-to-station or station-to-work/final destination trip. Shuttles are often tailored to a specific niche market, the most common being commuters traveling to and from major employment centers.

Over two dozen shuttle applications were identified in the case studies and research. Unlike circulators, which were categorized by operating characteristics—fixed route, route deviation, and demand response—shuttles have been categorized by trip purpose:

- Rail station to employment center,
- Residence to regional bus or rail, or
- Midday employee shuttles.

Rail Station to Employment Center Shuttles

The first category of shuttles is those that connect regional rail stations to employment destinations. By creating this link in the network, transit becomes a more attractive and viable alternative to the single-occupant automobile for choice riders and provides mobility and increased employment opportunities for transit dependents. Examples of this type of service include:

- Route 960, Bishop Ranch, CCCTA;
- Route 991, Concord Station, CCCTA;
- Sorrento Valley Coaster, San Diego Transit;
- Merrit 7 Commuter Connection, Norwalk (CT) Transit District;
- Virgin Atlantic Commuter Connection, Norwalk (CT) Transit District;
- Centennial Avenue Shuttle, NJ Transit;
- Convent Station Shuttle, NJ Transit; and
- Shoreline East Connection, Connecticut Transit.

Definition

Regular transit is often supplemented by a special short shuttle route, which provides connectivity between key locations served by the longer-haul network. The service design is based on short routes offering direct, quick travel times between start and end points, a schedule coordinated with the regional network, and an attractive fare policy. The emphasis on direct connections from origin to destination distinguishes shuttles from circulators, which, although providing shuttle components in many cases, generally have more circuitous, less time-sensitive route designs serving multiple trip purposes and destinations.

A combined regional rail and shuttle program is aimed at getting choice riders out of their cars and at providing increased mobility to nonchoice riders; as such, the travel time and cost characteristics need to be tailored to be competitive with automobile travel times and cost (Figure 42).

Shuttles are commonly used in both urban and suburban settings. An urban rail example is the Times Square-Grand Central Shuttle in New York City, connecting north/south services on the east and west sides of Manhattan. In the suburban setting, shuttles commonly connect rail stations to major employment destinations located outside walking distance from the station but not more than approximately 15 min away. The eight examples of these services described from the case studies and research are identified in the list given in the previous section.

Applicability

The key to the application of rail station (or bus terminal, although none were identified in the case studies) to work shuttles is to apply them in situations where the market can support the services and where the combined transit trip—home to regional rail, regional rail, regional rail to work—can be competitive with the same trip made by single-occupant vehicle.

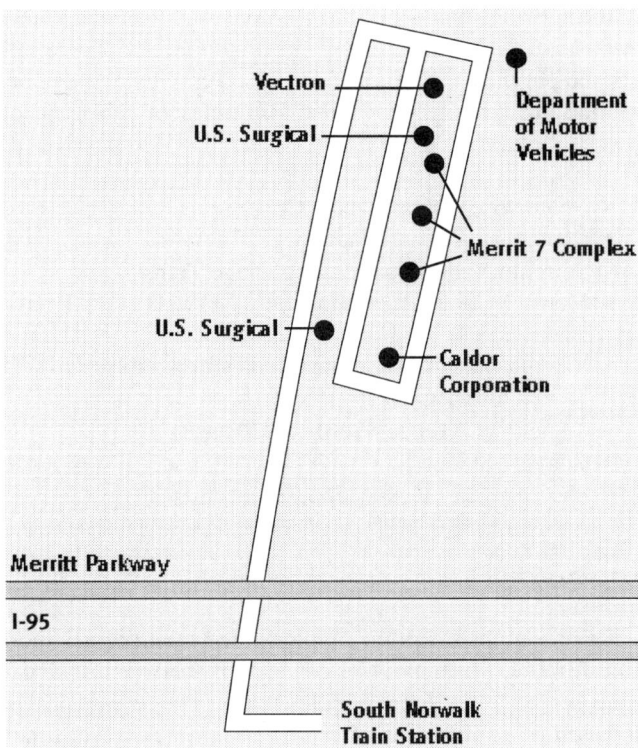

Figure 42. Norwalk Commuter Connection links Metro-North rail service to a 13,000-person regional employment center.

This does not mean that the trip time needs to be shorter or cost less than for automobile travel. The trip may in fact be slightly longer and possibly the same price, but other factors will come into play—consistent travel times unaffected by potential highway congestion, accidents, and so forth; comfort and the opportunity to read, sleep, or relax while on the train; less wear and tear on a personal vehicle (or even one less vehicle required in a household); and the intangible benefit of contributing to a better environment.

Based on a review of the services offered, the following are the most relevant conditions for application of shuttle services:

- There must be a concentrated employment base, with a significant percentage of the jobs located outside of walking distance from regional transit, and there must be a regional rail or bus presence in the area, with a significant station or transfer terminal having a reasonable level of service during peak periods. The shuttle service requires both to be successful. Experience has shown that a station with minimal peak service for inbound employees does not offer enough scheduling flexibility, even with a good shuttle program, and an area that has a low employment base, or where most employment is concentrated around the station, cannot generate enough riders.
- The employment targets should be outside of walking distance but not so far that the shuttle trip itself becomes a major part of the overall trip. The bulk of the commuter trip should be on the regional rail or express bus system and not on shuttles using local roadways.
- The regional transit network interfacing with the shuttle service must serve origin-destination patterns that meet the origin-destination patterns of a reasonable number of employees in the area. With trip making becoming increasingly diverse, it is essential to determine whether, for any given set of work sites, a sufficient number of workers come from origins along the rail or bus lines a shuttle would serve.
- The attraction of rail shuttles and transit is greater in areas where highway congestion makes peak-period commuting difficult or where parking is either fully utilized or expensive. In such environments, a well-designed service can provide competitive travel times and costs to go along with the potential for better travel time reliability, comfortable seats, and a relaxing trip.
- Shuttles are more applicable in areas where there are a few major employers who are willing to provide sponsorship and possible financial backing for the service. Areas with high employment but few major employers appear to have a lower probability for success, independent of other considerations such as congestion or parking issues.

The shuttles described in the case studies serve employers in edge cities, both within the city center and along major employment corridors, with commuters usually traveling in both directions, for example, the traditional CBD-oriented peak direction as well as the off-peak reverse commute direction. Other shuttles serve exurban employment enclaves, designed to serve reverse commuters to these remote locations.

Performance Range

Employment shuttles by their nature serve niche markets; that is, a small portion of the total travel market commuting to any one location. Thus, on a regional basis the number of trips as a percentage of all trips is rather small; the key is to capture a reasonable mode share of the trips that originate within the corridor served by regional bus or rail. As an example, the total employment market in New Haven, Connecticut, is 85,000 persons, and 58,000 work within the CBD, an area served by the Shoreline East Shuttle. However, further stratification based on home origin within the Shoreline East service territory and the number of people who can walk from the train to the station reveals that only 2,500 of the 85,000 persons are truly within the potential market for the rail shuttle program. Thus, the ridership in 1995 of 425 trips per day or 212 individuals calculates to a mode share of over 8 percent of the market using the shuttle.

This immediately provides two conclusions regarding expectations and performance:

- Shuttle services have to be viewed in their context, as niche services, when policy makers review their record and daily ridership figures, which range from 45 to 637 for the eight services reviewed in this research effort. These shuttles have to be carefully tailored to the employment patterns of their respective areas to be successful. Furthermore, they need to be viewed in the context of overall regional congestion management strategies and regulations as a piece of a larger puzzle encompassing other transit and TDM actions.
- Shuttle programs have to be carefully designed and tailored to the markets they serve in order to be effective. Given their relatively small markets, they have to have hours and headways tailored to the travel patterns of the local market and cannot overextend schedules; they also must find cost-effective ways to operate.

Creative public-private partnerships are behind the success of two shuttles in Contra Costa County (Table 7). Route 960 connects the Walnut Creek BART station to Bishop Ranch Business Park (Figure 43) Bishop Ranch is one of the Bay Area's premier edge cities, a mammoth 585-acre master-planned office-industrial campus, with over 60,000 on-site employees. Using money from a mitigation fund to ease the disruptive effects of retrofitting a critical freeway interchange in the county, CalTrans joined with the Sunset Development Corporate (the owner of Bishop Ranch) to sponsor the 960 Express Shuttle. Employees of Bishop Ranch ride free by displaying an identification badge, and the general public pays a $1.25 fare. The 960 Express Shuttle's fixed-route predecessor carried only 6.7 passengers per hour. In late-1995, the Express Shuttle averaged 15.8 passengers per revenue hour. Its monthly ridership jumped from 2,200 passengers in February 1995 to 6,000 6 months later. On some mornings, the load factor approaches 1.5. Because of ridership gains, the Express Shuttle's operating subsidy per passenger has fallen from $3.47 in 1994 to less than $2 in mid-1996. The express service also seems to have helped meet air-quality goals. The Bay Area's air-quality management district has assigned Bishop Ranch a 0.80 target for its vehicle employee ratio (VER) — the number of vehicles used for commuting divided by the number of employees. In 1994, Bishop Ranch's VER was around 0.90, but with the stepped-up Route 960 service, it fell to 0.81 in mid-1995.

A similar express shuttle service, Route 991, connects BART's Concord station to three business parks — Chevron U.S.A., Concord Airport Plaza, and Galaxy Office Park (Figure 44). Employers at these office parks help underwrite the cost of these peak-hour-only shuttle runs. They agreed to do so as a condition to receiving building permits. Their employees ride free by flashing a shuttle card or an employee ID; all others pay regular fares. The operating subsidy per passenger trip is around $2.55, in large part because most patrons pay no fare; still, this is well below CCCTA's standard of $3.80 per passenger trip. All three business parks are satisfied with Route 991's performance and plan to more aggressively market the service to on-site employees in coming years.

Another example of an express shuttle from a rail stop to a massive suburban job concentration is San Diego's Sorrento Valley Coaster Connection. Sorrento Valley, located near the junction of I-5 and I-805, has some 70,000 employees, mostly housed in campus-style office parks. There are more jobs at this location than in downtown San Diego. The campus-style settings, combined with the valley's hilly terrain, make the area ill-suited to conventional fixed-route services. In 1995, CMAQ funds were used to operate vans, contracted from private operators, that provide door-to-door connections from a commuter rail station on the Coast Express Rail (The Coaster) in north San Diego to the Sorrento Valley. The service has been hugely successful, with daily ridership growing from 450 a day in mid-1995 to a high of 630 passengers a day in November 1995. This results in an operating cost of around $3.35 per passenger trip. The contractor charges $30.50 per vehicle hour to provide the service. Users ride free

TABLE 7 Operating Performance of Rail Station to Employment Center Shuttles

Service	Program	Passengers per Day	Passengers per Hour	Cost per Trip	Cost Recovery
Rte. 960, Bishop Ranch	CCCTA		15.8	Under $ 2.00	
Rte. 991, Concord	CCCTA	80		$ 2.55	
Sorrento Valley Coaster	San Diego	637		$ 3.35	
Merrit 7	Norwalk Transit (CT)	60	10.0 (est)	$ 4.00 (est)	
Virgin Atlantic	Norwalk Transit (CT)	45	7.5 (est)	$ 5.30 (est)	
Centennial Ave.	NJ Transit	78			30.2%
Convent Station	NJ Transit	73			30.8%
Shoreline East	CT Transit	425	28.8	$ 2.05	

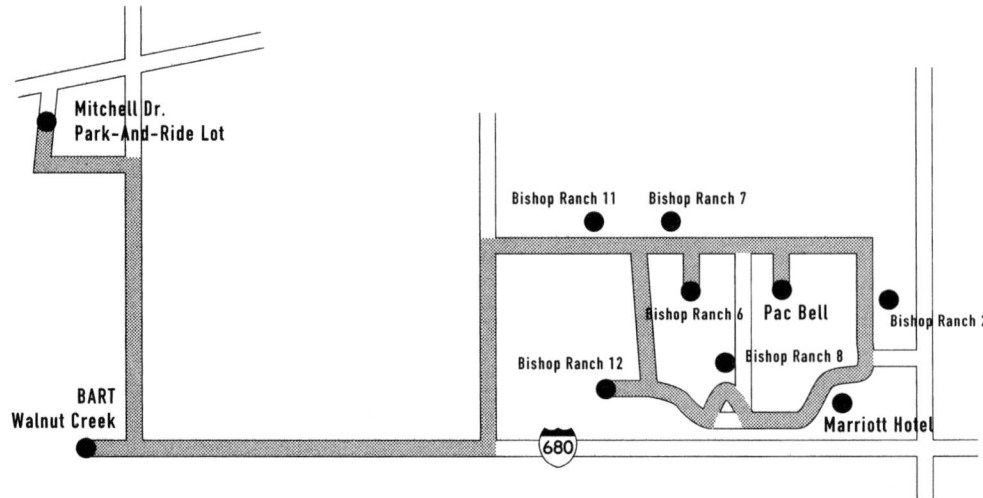

Figure 43. Route 960 Express Shuttle connects the Walnut Creek BART Station to the 585-acre Bishop Ranch, which has over 60,000 on-site employees, in Central Costa County, California.

by showing a monthly pass. Virtually all customers are middle-income "choice" riders who would otherwise solo commute to work, particularly in view of the fact that they could park for free at their workplaces. Despite the program's popularity and support, future funding is uncertain once CMAQ funds end in February 1997. The Metropolitan Transportation Development Board, one of the program sponsors, will extend the service another year if employers pay half the cost; however, many of the employers think tax dollars they pay to the county should finance the service just as other programs are financed. The San Diego Association of Governments is seeking a compromise arrangement that would combine public funds, employer contributions, and a fare, but the North County Transit District, where the service operates, does not want to introduce a fare, believing the Coaster fare is sufficient. A coordinating committee was set up to negotiate the issues in an attempt to reach an agreement to continue the service, which all believe is a major success.

Several shuttles from rail stations to local employers have been developed on the East Coast. Experiences with the Metro North Railroad and Shoreline East in Connecticut and with NJ Transit rail are described here.

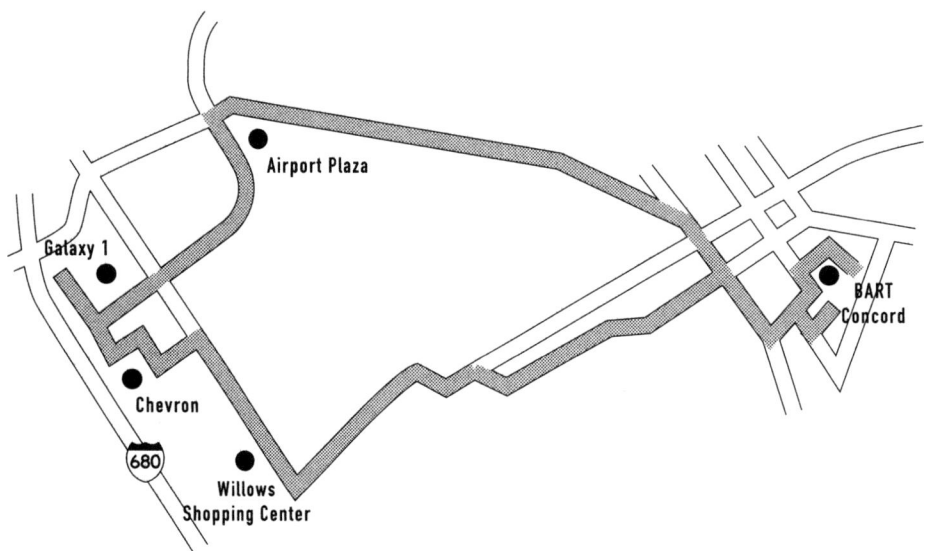

Figure 44. Route 991 Concord Commuter Express in Central Costa County connects BART to three business parks, which partially underwrite the cost of the service.

Shuttle services from rail stations to local employers are provided in New Haven, Stamford, Norwalk, and Greenwich under the banner of the "Commuter Connection" (Figure 45) Operations are provided by the local bus operator—the Norwalk Transit District in Norwalk and Greenwich and Connecticut Transit in New Haven and Stamford, with funding from the Connecticut DOT. The most successful of the programs is the Shoreline East shuttle, which connects the Shoreline East rail service terminus in New Haven to downtown New Haven employers and which serves commuters from suburban communities to the east. The shuttles carry 425 passengers a day according to 1995 statistics, operating for the most part during peak periods. The productivity is 28.8 passengers per hour, at a cost of $2.05 per trip. The cost per trip is relatively high given the productivity of the service because it is operated with regular CT Transit equipment and operators, at a cost of $58.95 per hour. The volumes are such that full-sized transit coaches are needed during the peak of the peak; CT Transit achieves some economies in the operation by interlining equipment with regular routes, thus keeping excess hours down. The performance of the service is exceptional, and several factors apparently contribute:

- The shuttle and rail service were implemented at the same time, which helped the operators to shape travel patterns and habits from the outset.
- Having been designed as a unit, the schedules are fully coordinated with very easy transfers from the train to the bus.
- The shuttle is free for monthly rail pass holders, so there is no reason not to use the bus because it is always there and waiting.
- Most employment locations in New Haven—Yale University, the medical establishment, Southern New England Telephone—are not easily reached from the station on foot.
- The congestion on I-95, which parallels the Shoreline East, is very bad with major queues at a bridge crossing into New Haven; this affords rail service a true competitive edge, which, when coupled with the free fare and seamless transfer, makes the combination very attractive to choice riders.
- The local Transportation Management Association, Regional Planning Agency, Connecticut DOT, and operators have collectively worked with the community, done planning and outreach, and heavily marketed the program directly to employers and potential riders.

The Norwalk shuttles operate in a far more modest environment and have correspondingly lower ridership and productivity levels. Whereas New Haven has a history of transit use dating back to the trolley car era, Norwalk is largely an automobile-oriented community with no strong history of transit use. As the suburban communities along the shoreline of Connecticut have become major residential and employment centers, traffic congestion along the two principal east-west roadways has increased. As these roadways parallel the Metro North rail line from New Haven to New York, the opportunity to divert some automobile travelers to the rail service was identified by state and local planners and transit operators. The Merritt 7 shuttle serves a large corporate park and employment corridor about 5 mi (8 km) north of South Norwalk Station, accessible to the station in part by a limited access connector to I-95. Since its implementation, the service has a steady but small ridership, which reached about 60 trips per day in 1996. Service is provided by the NTD at a cost per hour of $40.00, and the cost per trip is about $4.00.

A second route to the same general area but serving the northern end of the corridor was dropped in 1996 because of poor ridership. Apparent reasons included long travel times, dispersed employment locations, and poor employer support. The resources from this service were recently transferred to another area of the community, serving Norwalk Hospital and Virgin Atlantic Airlines, which is new to the community. Ridership is currently about 45 passenger trips per day, at a cost of $5.53 per trip. A concern of the system is that over time the Virgin Atlantic work force will relocate to the Norwalk area and that the shuttle will no longer be an option for these employees.

Shuttle services in Norwalk do not achieve high levels of use. One reason may be that passengers have to pay a fare, either a discounted fare as part of a Uniticket with Metro North or through the farebox. Other reasons are that most commuter patterns were set a long time before the shuttle was introduced, that congestion is still not seen as a major barrier for most people, and that parking is still free. Lastly, the total size of the market is far smaller than in New Haven, Bishop Ranch, and Concord.

The two NJ Transit shuttles were developed as part of the agency's experimental services program. The Convent Station route operates in the edge city of Morristown, and the Centennial Avenue shuttle connects that employment corridor to the New Brunswick station located a few miles away. Both

Figure 45. The name "Commuter Connection" is used throughout Connecticut by operators providing rail shuttle links to Metro-North as part of the Connecticut DOT efforts to promote transit options to suburban work sites.

services have similar daily ridership of 73 to 78 trips per day and cost recovery rates of 30.5 percent, above NJ Transit's standard for success of 25 percent. The New Brunswick service also draws riders from local buses and walk-in riders from neighborhoods in the city.

The performance of the rail shuttles for employment connections suggests that these can be very effective, targeted services that supplement regional transit services and support regional congestion mitigation strategies. In most cases, riders using the shuttle are new users of the rail system and therefore bring additional revenues to the regional rail or bus network at no additional cost; in this context, their subsidies overstate their true economic benefit to the transportation infrastructure, which is an important policy consideration for those providing such services.

Conditions of Effectiveness

The basic conditions of applicability pertaining to the background environment, service design, and policy and support were discussed in the section on applicability. A more specific list of factors that appear to be important determinants of success or failure, identified through the case studies, are discussed in this section.

Background Environment. The two basic conditions for applicability are the presence of a concentrated employment base and an active intermodal transfer center. However, even with these two conditions in place, other factors pertaining to them influence performance.

- The employment market may be large, but the potential travel market still needs to be determined. Specifically, the origin-destination patterns served by the regional bus and/or rail network must serve the origins of a sufficient number of those individuals working in the target area. Second, the employment market must not be entirely concentrated around the station within walking distance or far enough to make the shuttle trip excessively long. Finally, the presence of a few major employers supporting the service, either monetarily or with benefit programs to employees—subsidized transit fares, guaranteed ride home, flex-time—provides a solid base from which to develop a successful program.
- Parking at the origin end of the trip is a significant factor. Those interested in switching to rail and shuttle from automobile must be able to park at their home station. Availability is more critical than the price of parking; without the certainty of being able to park every day, potential users will not use the new service.
- Traffic congestion on parallel roadways is a strong incentive to use a well-designed service that will save time, provide a more reliable trip on a daily basis, and be more relaxing. Pricing or restricted parking at the work destination could have a similar effect but is not highly utilized among the cases studied.

Service Design. Success is predicated upon having a well-designed shuttle service that is attractive to automobile commuters. The key is to remember that the service is competing with the automobile trip and the comforts and perceived, if not real, convenience of automobile travel. Key service design features must emphasize comfort, convenience, and reliability.

- First and foremost, the routes have to be well-designed. They must be as direct as possible between the transfer point and each key employment destination. To the extent possible, they should drop commuters at the front door and not at the end of a long driveway or at curbside when there are significant setbacks. In-vehicle travel time needs to be minimized, with the shuttle portion of the total travel time not exceeding 25 percent. Experience suggests that, in real terms, trips of over 15 min are seldom attractive.
- The shuttle program should use comfortable vehicles and only in the case of very short trips should passenger loads exceed seating capacity. There are examples of systems using regular transit vehicles successfully (Shoreline East) or having standing loads (Bishop Ranch) but these are exceptions to the rule. Shoreline East was implemented in concert with rail to a new market rather than introduced later when travel patterns were already set, and Bishop Ranch's overloading is a condition of its successful ridership growth and not of its initial design and will be remedied over time with additional capacity.
- The shuttles and regional rail and bus need to have coordinated schedules, with timed transfers that minimize wait times. Travelers should be able to step off the regional service and directly into the shuttle. In the evening the shuttle should arrive back at the station about 5 min before the train. Attractive shuttle stops at the transfer point, with shelter for inclement weather, should be provided.
- Reliability is very important to commuters. Knowing the service will be there, but more important knowing that the trip each day will be about the same length, is a key selling point vis-a-vis automobile travel, especially along congested regional highways. Thus, operators need to provide reliable services and then market them extensively. Three elements can contribute greatly to the reliability and perception of reliability of shuttle service. First, having shuttle vehicles waiting for the train, rather than customers waiting for the shuttle, promotes the idea of easy transfers, service that is there when you want it, and high quality. This requires building sufficient layover time into the schedule. Second, most successful shuttles offer extra early morning, late morning, and/or late evening runs, recognizing that people do not always

work the same hours each day and that they need to know they can get home in the evening if they work a little late. These trips often have low ridership but provide benefits beyond the numbers in terms of obtaining a commitment from commuters to the service. Successful services are also backed up by guaranteed ride home services or emergency midday services, usually provided by the employers.
- Integrated fare policies positively influence ridership. Shuttles subsidized by one or more employers are offered free to employees of participating firms. Others are included in the price of a monthly commuter pass for the rail system, or for a small increment, and are accessed by flashing the monthly pass.

Policy and Support. A number of additional factors enable systems to be successful.

Planners and policy makers need to have realistic objectives and standards for shuttles, just as for other suburban mobility initiatives. These services are designed for a niche market and need to be judged on their cost-effectiveness and contribution to congestion mitigation as a single tool among many. They cannot be judged by sheer numbers compared with mainline, core services; they can be judged on their contribution to congestion mitigation on a corridor- or market-specific basis.

Shuttles accrue more revenue and ridership to the region than simply those attributed to the service itself. In most cases, except where there are walk-ins, shuttle users have paid for a trip on a regional service; thus shuttles increase productivity and cost-effectiveness for regional networks at a marginal cost, because they increase the number of passengers without requiring additional services.

As with all suburban options, the use of contractors or reduced labor rates to keep costs down and thus cost-effectiveness reasonable compared with other elements is important when dealing with low ridership services. Where costs are high, such as in Connecticut for Shoreline East, they are matched by high productivity; in New Jersey, more modest productivities are acceptable because low operating costs achieved through contracting enable many services to exceed the required cost recovery standard of 25 percent.

Employer-supported services have the best record of success, often because employers contribute to the operating cost, ensuring continued service and demonstrating commitment to their employees.

All the programs are marketed extensively, both by the transit operator and by employers. Route maps and schedules are distributed at employment sites, along with special shuttle materials, free rides are offered as promotions upon initiation for up to 3 months in some cases, and trip itineraries are developed for interested users. Marketing usually is a joint effort of transit operators, employers, and transportation management associations.

Supportive programs and regulations can boost the market for shuttles. Parking restrictions on employers, Clean Air Act regulations, and local congestion mitigation regulations are all examples of mandated regulatory support that requires that employers participate in regional efforts to move commuters from the car to public transportation.

Residence to Regional Bus or Rail Shuttles

The second category of shuttles is those operated from a residential neighborhood to a regional transit center. Three methods are used to provide these services—dial-a-ride, fixed route, and route deviation (called "Flex-Routes" in New Jersey, from where the route deviation examples were taken). These services provide transit opportunities in neighborhoods where conventional fixed-route services do not work because of terrain, density, or an inability to compete favorably with automobile travel. Examples of this type of service include:

- Paradise Hills, San Diego Transit (SDT);
- Mira Mesa, SDT;
- Mid City, SDT;
- Rancho Bernardo, SDT;
- Scripps Ranch, SDT;
- Friendship Express, LANTA;
- Walnut Creek, CCCTA;
- Moreno Valley, Riverside Transit;
- Shuttles 1,4,5, LANTA;
- Lawrence Flex-Route, NJ Transit; and
- West Windsor Flex-Route, NJ Transit.

Definition

The shuttles within this category provide services in residential areas that link to the regional network. Services are provided to rail stations, bus transfer facilities, and, in some cases, malls or downtowns. The key is to make the combined shuttle/regional transit trip attractive, particularly to choice riders who currently make the trip by automobile. Thus, travel time and costs need to be tailored to be competitive, special conditions need to be exploited, and service quality needs to be high.

Applicability

Residence-based shuttles are implemented to connect regional rail or bus services to a local community. Based on the case studies, there are two distinct situations under which these services are applied:

- In areas where public transportation mobility is an objective of local planners and operators but where regular fixed-route bus services would not be practical because of terrain, modest demand is unsuitable to

regular service, or in areas where the street network makes fixed-route service impractical.
- In areas having special conditions related to traffic congestion, parking availability, or other factors associated with utilizing the regional transit service that require a short, direct, and timely peak-hour connection but not necessarily all day service.

Applicability requires the presence of a good regional network with which to connect, a reasonable-sized market that can be served efficiently with fixed-route or demand response services, and an ability to create a public transportation service that can compete with the automobile.

The key to the application is to design a service that offers choice users some advantage over the use of their automobile and provides mobility for transit dependents beyond the local neighborhood. Applications of these shuttles aimed at the choice rider—for example, in middle- and upper-income locations for trips to regional rail or express bus—function best where the reliability or speed of the automobile trip is constrained by congestion or pricing. Applications for the transit-dependent market work best in moderate-density environments where there are a lot of fixed-route choices at the transfer location; the emphasis for these riders is less on speed, although that is still a factor, than on mobility—the chance to get to many locations throughout the service area.

Performance Range

There are seven demand response/dial-a-ride shuttles in this group, four fixed-route shuttles, and two route deviation shuttles. They have a wide variation in performance ranges among them and are best discussed within the three individual operating categories.

Demand Response Shuttles. The demand response shuttles operate in the most difficult terrain and, in many cases, the least densely populated areas. They are designed to provide shuttle connections to regional services where fixed-route service cannot.

Within this group, most of the services are provided by San Diego Transit. DART is a demand responsive program established in 1982 by San Diego Transit. It offers local service and connections to fixed-route services in communities where conventional fixed-route services are not effective. Target communities have one or more of the following features:

- Discontinuous street network,
- Canyon terrain,
- Low transit demand,
- Geographic isolation, and
- Dispersed travel patterns.

DART was designed to be an extension of fixed-route service in these target areas. Passengers make reservations at least 1 hour in advance of when they want to get to the transfer location. More than one-half of DART riders have standing reservations. The priority for trips is the transfer trip, although other intercommunity trips will be provided as space and time allow. DART operates from 5:00 AM to 8:00 PM. The base fare is $1.75 with a free transfer to an outbound bus, and $0.50 with a bus transfer on an inbound trip or monthly pass (in either direction).

DART service is currently provided in five communities:

1. ***Paradise Hills***—This community in southeast San Diego is characterized by a discontinuous street network and hilly terrain; moreover, much of the demand was for service to the neighboring jurisdictions of National City and Chula Vista, which are outside the San Diego Transit service area. DART service was introduced in 1982, a year after fixed-route service was discontinued because of operating inefficiencies. DART vehicles provide circulation within Paradise Hills and offer connections to bus routes operated by San Diego Transit and the two neighboring jurisdictions.
2. ***Mira Mesa***—DART provides connections to three San Diego Transit express routes destined for downtown San Diego in this rapidly growing community about 20 mi (32 km) to the north. Although the population density in Mira Mesa could support fixed-route service, the limited through-street access would make conventional transit operations inefficient.
3. ***Mid City***—DART provides connections to eight bus routes in this transit-dependent area just north of San Diego's central city. Although San Diego Transit provides extensive service along Mid City's arterial roads, the street network is broken up by canyons and does not allow adequate local circulation. DART was initially introduced to replace a portion of a fixed route operating within the community.
4. ***Rancho Bernardo***—DART was introduced to provide local connections to express services in this affluent community in the I-15 corridor. Despite strong political support, the service has not attracted commuters; most passengers are elderly residents making local shopping and medical trips. San Diego Transit had previously discontinued fixed-route service in this community because of complaints about noise.
5. ***Scripps Ranch***—DART service was introduced to this area in the I-15 corridor in an attempt to encourage residents to patronize express bus services. Like Rancho Bernardo, Scripps Ranch is fairly affluent with a low population density; thus far, most DART riders are making local school trips.

Startup funding for the first three DART services (Paradise Hills, Mira Mesa, Mid City) came from an FTA Section 6 demonstration grant. San Diego Transit assumed funding responsibility when the demonstration period ended. Service in Rancho Bernardo and Scripps Ranch is funded by local sales tax revenues dedicated to new transit services.

DART service is provided through a contractual arrangement between San Diego Transit and a private operator. The current contractor provides a fleet of 19 vehicles with two spares. Most are 8-passenger Chevrolet Astro Vans. The fleet also includes four 12-passenger lift-equipped vans. San Diego Transit reimburses the contractor at a fixed rate per vehicle service hour ($15.71) and vehicle service mile ($0.17). Combined hourly cost averages $17.75. The contract provides an incentive for achieving a farebox recovery ratio of 20 percent or greater. San Diego Transit pays the operator 50 percent of fare revenues above this minimum level; a ceiling limits the maximum bonus to 4 percent of total annual contract cost. In addition, if the average number of passengers per vehicle service hour drops below five, the contractor is required to reduce vehicle assignments.

DART services carried over 232,000 passengers in FY 1995 at an average of 0.32 passenger per mile. The services had a cost per trip of $4.92 and a subsidy per passenger of $3.74. The cost recovery ratio was 23.9 percent. In comparison, the fixed-route bus services averaged 2.53 passengers per mile, $1.58 per passenger trip, and $0.84 subsidy per trip and had a 46.5 percent cost recovery ratio. The DART program, operated by contractors, had a cost per mile of only $1.83, less than one-half the fixed-route cost of $3.99; this competitive pricing advantage, coupled with the premium DART fare, allows DART to have a cost recovery rate about one-half that of fixed-route bus, despite having a productivity one tenth that of fixed-route service.

Among the demand response services, the range of performance varies (Table 8). The three best performing services are Paradise Hills, Mira Mesa, and Mid City. Scripps Ranch performs more modestly, with a reasonable cost recovery ratio compared with the other three but lower productivity and total ridership. Rancho Bernardo carries about the same number of passengers per mile as Scripps Ranch but at a significantly higher cost per trip and lower farebox recovery ratio. Rancho Bernardo and Scripps Ranch services were community initiated and have a lower core of riders who have successfully advocated these services in their communities. The other three have a broader spectrum of support and more favorable operating circumstances.

Paradise Hills has a great deal of demand for service into neighboring National City and Chula Vista; the service replaced a discontinued fixed-route service and makes connections to SDT buses and to buses from the two communities. Mira Mesa is a rapidly growing suburb about 20 mi (32 km) north of San Diego. The DART service connects to three express routes. Mid City connects to eight SDT bus routes. It serves a heavily transit-dependent area adjacent to the San Diego CBD in an area where the arterial network is broken by canyon terrain and local circulation for fixed-route buses was discontinued in a portion of the community. Rancho Bernardo, on the other hand, is an affluent community in the I-15 corridor. Despite strong political support, the service has not attracted commuters; most riders are making local trips, which was not the original objective for the service. Scripps Ranch is a connector to express bus services, again in an affluent area of the region. Very few commuters use the service; a market has developed for local circulation for school trips.

The Friendship Express is a very small program, offered by LANTA on Saturdays between suburban Bath and the Whitehall Mall, using a LANTA Metro Plus van. The service is extremely limited as a general public link; non-Metro Plus riders need to reserve a trip at least 2 days in advance and must go to a designated stop location in the community identified by LANTA. At Whitehall Mall, free transfers are available to other LANTA buses. No ridership statistics were available for this service.

CCCTA ran the final shuttle among this group in Walnut Creek. The program lasted 3 years, ending in July 1995. Described as a collection of "flex-vans," residents from a busy corridor were delivered directly to the Walnut Creek BART station, door-to-door, during peak commuter hours in the morning and afternoon/evening. Afternoon headways

TABLE 8 DART Service Performance Statistics in San Diego

Area	Cost per Mile	Passengers per Mile	Cost per Trip	Subsidy per Trip	Farebox Recovery
Paradise Hills	$1.45	0.32	$4.59	$3.35	26.9%
Mira Mesa	$1.59	0.34	$4.65	$3.52	24.2%
Mid City	$1.83	0.37	$4.99	$3.79	24.1%
Scripps Ranch	$1.39	0.23	$6.06	$4.84	20.0%
Rancho Bernardo	$1.75	0.22	$8.16	$7.21	11.6%
TOTAL	$1.58	0.32	$4.92	$3.74	23.9%
Fixed Route Local	$3.99	2.53	$1.58	$0.84	46.5%

were 20 min for returning passengers. Reservations were required for the mornings only and could be made up to 1 hour in advance of the trip. Daily ridership in 1993 was 32 passengers and grew to 47 in 1994. The farebox recovery rate was 5.2 percent in 1993 and 8.6 percent in 1994. The subsidy per trip was $9.81 in 1993 and $7.85 in 1994. The high deficit per trip coupled with scheduling difficulties that limited productivity led to cancelation of the program, despite the high degree of customer satisfaction among those who used it. The Link served a middle- and upper-income neighborhood, and critics among others in the County resented the high subsidies for these residents when there were other service needs in the community.

Demand response shuttles clearly are difficult to operate at reasonable cost-efficiencies. Those that are more productive generally operate in more dense neighborhoods than those that are not and have a larger number of transit-dependent individuals residing in the service area. Those that operate in middle- and upper-income areas do not compete well enough with the automobile to attract a large enough core of riders to make the services effective. In combination, low densities and high incomes have been a severe impediment to success despite well-designed and personalized service plans and low operating costs achieved through contracting.

Fixed-Route Shuttles. Four fixed-route shuttles were identified in the case studies: one in Riverside and three in Allentown.

Riverside Transit Authority (RTA) Route 16 service provides intermodal feeder service between the rapidly expanding Moreno Valley community and Metrolink. RTA initiated express service to Metrolink in response to congestion on the Moreno Freeway. The service attracts riders bound for suburban San Bernardino County as well as Los Angeles. Pickups at the Moreno Valley Mall provide plentiful free parking as an informal park-and-ride. The shuttle portion of this route is operated during peak periods; during the remainder of the day Route 16 provides regular fixed-route local bus service within Moreno County. Route 16 METRO Express, as the peak service is called, is a limited-stop shuttle to the downtown Riverside terminal, which offers transfers to rail and almost all RTA bus routes. The feeder element, begun in 1993, is timed to meet METROLINK trains. There are eight rail-oriented shuttle runs a day, meeting five inbound and three outbound trains each day. For the last 6 months of 1995, ridership for the morning feeder averaged 7 passengers per run, and afternoon runs averaged 11 passengers. Fares are integrated with RTA and METROLINK fares.

LANTA operates five shuttles in addition to the WhirleyBird as part of its suburban mobility strategy adopted in the 1993 Strategic Plan. Of the five, two run from downtown Allentown and do reverse commuter services and thus are not a focus for this project. The other three provide connections from surrounding suburban communities to major activity centers and to centers that have connections to LANTA fixed routes. Union support for the program has allowed LANTA to use differential shuttle operator rates that have kept costs down while keeping the program in-house with the operators union. LANTA had a suburban performance standard of 12.5 passengers per hour for FY 1995, which was increased because of financial constraints to 15.0 as of June 1996. Overall, the shuttles average 10.5 passengers per hour, with the WhirleyBird the highest at 21.0 and the three described in this section ranging from 6.0 to 15.0. Thus, none are currently meeting the standard for performance and they are in the process of being reviewed for continuation.

As with the demand response services, these fixed-route shuttles are heavily influenced by the size of the market and relative convenience of the competing automobile trip. In LANTA, the markets are relatively small and the automobile is highly competitive. Therefore, the services depend on the captive riders in the service area. Services have been carefully limited in scope to capture key elements of this market, with stops geared to two industrial parks and a training center in addition to the bus transfer points at the malls. The Moreno service operates in a more favorable circumstance. The market is larger, the linkage is to a rail line as well as local and express buses, and roadway congestion is significant. Coupled with a favorable income profile, these factors contribute to a moderately successful service.

Route Deviation Shuttle. Two shuttles provided in New Jersey connect residential neighborhoods to the very crowded Princeton Junction rail station, a major commuter stop in the Northeast corridor line serving New York, Philadelphia, and employment centers between in Metropark, New Brunswick, Newark, and Trenton, among others. The Princeton Junction station parking lots are at or above capacity with significant waiting lists, which restricts rail ridership, makes parking difficult for commuters going in during the late AM peak, and results in long walking distances from parking spaces to the platform. As part of its experimental services program, NJ Transit designed shuttle services from the two neighboring communities of Lawrence and East Windsor to increase the opportunities for rail commuting among non-rail users and possibly switch park-and-ride users to shuttle users, reducing parking demand and the need for costly parking expansion.

The concept selected for the services is called a flex route, which is a route deviation-type program. Routes were developed in the community, but passengers can either board at designated stops or request a doorstep pickup. In the afternoon, returning riders are offered the same option. As ridership patterns develop, NJ Transit hoped to reduce the need for deviations by adjusting the fixed routes to the demand. The services are operated by a private contractor. Fares are integrated with the rail fares. The Lawrence service is a tremendous success, with 152 passengers per day or 11.7 passengers per trip and a cost recovery of 69.3 percent. The West Windsor service is less successful, but at 19 percent cost recovery is still moving toward the threshold standard of 25 percent. It carries 31 passengers per day or 3.1 passengers per trip. Overall, the service carries over 180 passengers daily and therefore reduces parking demand by about 90 spaces. The exact number of new rail users versus previous park-and-rider users is unknown, but the service has certainly contributed to additional ridership and revenues for the rail program as well.

Conditions of Effectiveness

The success or failure of these services clearly depends on finding a very specific problem or need in the community and then designing a service around that need. Services implemented for general mobility purposes in areas without specific needs, and specifically without conditions inhibiting automobile use, have no record of success. The conditions for success and a discussion follow:

1. **Market Profile**—The market profile needs to be established when the service is set up, for example, is the service aimed at the choice rider or the transit dependent, or can it serve both? If it is the choice rider, the service must offer an advantage over the automobile; if it is the transit-dependent rider, the service should offer opportunities that maximize mobility throughout the service area. In either case, the number of potential users needs to be sufficiently large to provide a base from which to grow.
2. **Service Parameters**—Shuttle services need to be direct, transfers need to be timed, and schedules need to match rider needs. Choice riders using the service to link to commuter services generally need service for peak periods only, with some flexibility for early and later trips; services geared to the transit dependents and overall market should provide all day services.
3. **Income and Density**—Residential-based shuttles have not had a great deal of success among middle- and upper-income residents, particularly from low-density areas, unless there are special circumstances that make automobile travel difficult. On the other hand, applications in more moderate-density middle- and lower-middle income neighborhoods in San Diego performed better, where the services provided the transit mobility for the entire community and not solely for commuters.
4. **Congestion and Parking**—Traffic congestion, parking constraints, and parking rates are the three biggest influences that will support commuter-oriented shuttles in middle- and upper-income areas. The Lawrence and West Windsor shuttles demonstrate the potential for shuttles when the rail station parking situation is highly constrained. The Moreno Valley service demonstrates that shuttles can be successful for longer commutes when regional highways are heavily congested. Conversely, the experiences in San Diego in Rancho Bernardo and Scripps Ranch suggest that the automobile is still the preferred commuter option, despite growing roadway congestion. And in Westport, Connecticut, ridership on shuttles to train stations has constantly diminished since its inception in 1975 as more parking has become available, and pricing continues to favor park-and-ride.

Other factors discussed in other sections—maintaining cost-effectiveness through contracting, marketing, realistic objectives, and policy and regulatory support—play a role in achieving success with residential-based shuttles. But to be successful, there are two key determinants:

- For peak commuter-oriented shuttles, the service has to have greater appeal than the automobile.
- For all day services, the service area has to have a significant number of transit dependents, and the shuttle has to link the local area to the broader region to meet their travel needs.

Given either of these conditions, a well-designed and well-implemented project can produce the levels of performance demonstrated in the best of the case studies that, while far from those achieved with regular fixed-route services, still can meet regional objectives for cost-effectiveness and mobility.

Midday Employee Shuttles

Employers who encourage their workers to use transit have often provided a midday shuttle program, assuming that those who come to work without cars would like to get from the suburban office campus to local malls, restaurants, or downtowns for their lunch hour. Although some midday circulators have been successful—serving a broader market of workers and downtown shoppers, visitors, and so forth—the shuttles aimed almost exclusively to workers have failed consistently. Four midday employer shuttles were identified in the research. Examples of this type of service include:

- Bishop Ranch, CCCTA;
- Galleria, Houston METRO;
- Greenspoint, Houston METRO; and
- East Gate, NJ Transit.

Definition

As distinct from general circulators in activity centers, such as Route 103 in Contra Costa County, the midday employee shuttles are defined as short headway, short duration bus or van services designed to connect major employment sites with area restaurants, malls, or other activities that people would want to travel to during lunch. The services are generally provided at no fare and may be subsidized by employers. The market is the entire employment population, although the service was often initiated to give transit users a way to go out for lunch. This provides a dual objective—if successful, the service increases the attractiveness of transit as a commute option, and it reduces midday secondary travel.

The services are provided exclusively as fixed-route, fixed-schedule services so that employees can have a high sense of reliability and schedule certainty.

Applicability

Given that all four cases failed, the applicability of this concept appears to be limited; however, based on the design of the cases, it appears that the application requires the following:

- A very high density of employees;
- A concentrated set of midday destinations;
- A transit-friendly environment to promote ready access to and from designated stops;
- Short headways coupled with direct, short trips, so that workers can get out and back within their allotted lunch time, which may be as short as 45 to 60 mins;
- Reliable on-time performance, which may require a frequency of service of 5 min and which requires that traffic conditions be free-flowing;
- Free fare service; and
- Employer support, which may include flex-time to allow for midday trips, financial participation, or designated stop locations with street furniture at entrances.

Performance Range

The four services described have all been discontinued because of lack of use. The Bishop Ranch service was heavily supported, with private funding of $50,000 for operations for 1 year, a free fare, and active support. Despite having over 60,000 employees at this exurban enclave, the service produced only 420 per month; even with a private contractor providing the service, this translated to a cost of $10.00 per trip.

The Galleria and Greenpoint areas in Houston both had lunch shuttles that were dropped. These two edge city environments were not transit-friendly—it took too long to get to and from bus stops at the office settings that were served, the climate was often uncomfortable for waiting and walking, and the origins and destinations were difficult to serve efficiently.

The East Gate Industrial Park lunchtime shuttle was another of the NJ Transit experimental services. This service connected a major industrial park with a local commercial corridor. It was organized by NJ Transit and the regional TMA but had only lukewarm support from the employers at the site. The service was intended to complement a peak AM and PM shuttle program, offering transit users an option at lunch; that shuttle was subsequently abandoned because of low ridership, further eroding the potential ridership base. When discontinued, the midday service averaged less than one passenger trip per day, with a cost recovery rate of 1 percent.

Conditions of Effectiveness

Midday employee shuttles do not have a record of success as regularly operated transit service. Some employers have their own vans to move employees around between sites and occasionally provide trips to off-site locations. Caldor, Inc., in Connecticut has a van service between three buildings, for example, which also makes a stop at a local shopping center where their store is located.

Midday employee shuttles generally fail for any or all of the following reasons:

- The total travel time, including getting to the shuttle stop, waiting for the vehicle, in-vehicle time, and the reverse trip takes too long. Many employers offer lunch services on site in larger employment centers because it takes to long to go off site regardless of the mode. Even if it takes just as long to use an automobile, employees think they have more control over their schedule by using that mode.
- The environment has to be transit-friendly. Stops need to be convenient to entrances at work sites and at shopping/lunch sites. Shelters need to be provided for weather protection, and crosswalks or pedestrian overpasses may need to be provided in busy downtown locations.
- There may not be a market for the service because so few people come to work without cars, have free and ample parking, and have no compelling reason not to take a car out at lunch, for example, congested streets, parking charges.
- Even among those who use transit or carpool/vanpool to lunch, there may be no need for a shuttle to get out. Lunch pooling with automobile commuters is common and limits the needs of the nondriver for midday transit.

CHAPTER 5

SUBSCRIPTION BUSES AND VANPOOLS

Two subscription-based programs are offered to commuters—subscription buses/vans and vanpool programs.

SUBSCRIPTION BUSES

Subscription van and bus services, operated by private carriers, gained popularity in the 1970s by providing express bus services to communities generally unserved by regular transit. Subscription services focused on commuter markets, often from new communities such as Reston, Virginia, or Columbia, Maryland, providing service for the most part to downtown locations.

As the cost of these services escalated over time, many were taken over by transit operators and supported with subsidies. In many areas, regional growth brought a greater need for transit services to these markets, which led to the services being expanded and incorporated into the regular transit network.

Subscription bus or van services were not widely used among the case studies, and only two services were identified.

Description

Subscription services offer express bus services to a closed group of riders, identified by their affiliation to the sponsor of the service. Sponsors contract for the service with an operator at a set rate and offset that rate through the fares collected from subscribers or from their own resources. For example, an employer might pay one-half of the costs and obtain the other one-half from fares; a community board, condominium association, or the like might use assessment monies for a portion of the cost and fares from resident users for the remainder. In either case, the operator is assured of obtaining reimbursement for the full operating cost.

Subscription services offer regularity of supply and demand, for example, a schedule and route tailored to the subscribers' needs and the guarantee of a seat for each rider. Sponsors get a service tailored to their commuting needs, and operators get a service that minimizes unproductive operating miles and hours.

Public agencies have become a third participant in the provision of subscription services in recent years, working with local sponsors to develop and fund subscription services. In lieu of express or local bus services, which generally require a larger commitment of resources and have no assurance of success, operators have found that it is more economical to finance a portion of a subscription program in partnership with local sponsors. Thus, METRO in Houston has been willing to provide a subsidy per trip of $2.50 to interested sponsors, pegging this level of subsidy to the subsidy rate for its best third of park-and-ride services. LANTA subsidizes one-half the cost of its subscription van program, with the other 50 percent coming from employers and fares; the 50 percent recovery rate is well above that of the LANTA fixed-route program.

Applicability

Subscription buses are applicable in the following situations:

- Where there are a large number of individuals with common origins and destinations,
- Where there are common hours of travel, and
- Where there is an organization willing to sponsor the service.

These services have been started by employers, community organizations, and local governments where a common service pattern has been identified, where transit service can be competitive with automobile travel, and where commuters have expressed an interest in starting and using such a service. The Houston METRO project connects a residential suburb to an edge city; it creates a transit link that was not previously provided and an attractive alternative to the automobile. In Allentown, the LANTA program provides a link from the LANTA bus terminal downtown to a suburban industrial park. The service is designed to provide mostly transit-dependent individuals with the mobility needed to reach the growing suburban job market. By originating in downtown and providing free transfers to LANTA buses, it opens this opportunity to the entire area and creates a crosstown link that could not otherwise be created by direct bus service. (Many nonsubscription reverse bus services from downtown areas offer similar opportunities for crosstown trip making. Two successful examples are the reverse bus services operated by NJ Transit to Raritan Center from Newark and Irvington.)

Performance Range

There were only two services described in the case studies, one operated with buses and one with vans.

The Greenline Express in Houston is operated by a private contractor and connects the Kingswood park-and-ride lot in North Harris County with Greenspoint, a small edge city north of downtown Houston near the Intercontinental Airport (Figure 46). Sponsored by a group of Greenspoint businesses, the service carried about 340 passengers per month in 1995–96. The subsidy per trip of the service was $5.00, which is above the METRO standard of $2.50 for assuming operation of the service. METRO expects the subscription bus program over time will be a success. With additional employer participation and ridership, METRO is expecting the subsidy per trip to reach the standard. Because of the nature of the service, METRO also believes it will be able to allocate its resources more effectively among its many markets with tailored services such as these.

The Forks/Palmer Industrial Park subscription van provided by LANTA provides two morning and evening subscription runs from downtown Allentown, with timed transfers to all other LANTA bus routes. One-half of the operating costs are paid by LANTA, and the other one-half come from employers and fares. Fares are $12.50 for a 10-trip pass. As part of the service, passengers are also able to request an emergency ride home during the work day. When the service began, only a single passenger was using it. In mid-1996, there were 28 daily passengers on average, and the vans operated at a productivity of about 10 passengers per hour. The goal of 15 passengers per hour is set as the standard for LANTA's shuttles and special programs and is considered to be within reach for this program.

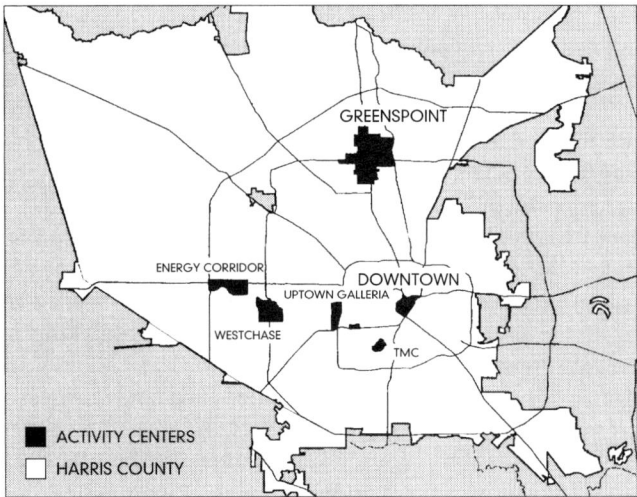

Figure 46. Edge cities in the Houston area, showing Greenspoint, the destination for the Greenline Express.

Conditions of Effectiveness

The development of subscription services depends entirely on identifying a sponsor willing to subsidize a portion of the operating cost, in concert with the public transit provider and fare-paying customers. Thus, this is the first condition that needs to be met to be successful with a subscription service.

Once a sponsor is identified and appropriate operating cost estimates and funding arrangements are made, the effectiveness of the service will be determined by the number of riders using it and the resulting subsidy per trip required for ongoing support. The following conditions will help support good ridership:

- Accurate estimates of the size of the market, taking into account common origins and destinations and times of travel;
- Discussions with potential riders to ensure that there is an interest in the service and to determine the characteristics of the service that will be most attractive to them;
- A service design that competes with automobile travel with respect to comfort, convenience, and travel time;
- Provision of a guaranteed ride home or emergency ride home program;
- Low operating costs to keep subsidy levels and fares at acceptable rates.

VANPOOLS

A number of transit properties offer vanpool services, nearly all of them focused on suburban commuting to large employment centers. In 1993, Seattle Metro operated over 500 vans, which represented almost 40 percent of all transit-agency sponsored vanpools around the country. The average publicly supported vanpool in 1993 recovered an estimated 60 percent of costs through fares, a high cost recovery ratio compared with most bus systems but substantially below the high levels of earlier decades when private subscription services often generated profits.

Two vanpool programs were identified in the case studies, in Fort Worth and Houston. They are briefly described in this section, along with a description of their performance.

Fort Worth has used CMAQ funds to underwrite vanpool fares. After the subsidy was introduced, the number of publically sponsored vans jumped from 39 to 81. These services have allowed the agency to eliminate eight costly and low ridership fixed-route bus runs that served Lockheed, one of the area's largest employers. The operating cost per passenger trip is far lower than for the previous bus service.

Houston's METROVan program started as a pilot program in 1994, although vanpools had flourished in the 1970s in the area. The vanpools are able to make use of an extensive HOV lane network, which has increased interest in them for commuting. As of 1995–96 there were 102 vanpools in service providing 34,400 monthly trips. Of the 102 vanpools, 33 were destined for the Galleria and 33 were to the TMC area, both suburban workplaces outside the Houston CBD (and shown in Figure 46). A few vans were also in use to exurban enclaves.

The METROVan program has been very successful in controlling operating subsidies and increasing mobility. The per passenger subsidy of $0.95 is considerably lower than the $1.92 subsidy per passenger for comparable park-and-ride bus services. METRO is considering opportunities to develop a new service with vanpools called Caravan. The aim is to coordinate vanpools with similar origins and destinations into a schedule that would imitate a bus service. Riders would have to be regularly assigned to one of the vans, but the opportunity to occasionally shift to another would offer people more flexibility and choice if they had to work late or come in early.

CHAPTER 6

SUMMARY: LESSONS AND CONCLUSIONS

The case experiences reviewed in this report provide useful policy insights about how future transit services might be designed to better serve suburban markets. Although generalizations are always at risk of oversimplifying matters, particularly given that serious responses to suburban growth are still largely embryonic, some patterns were nevertheless uncovered that provide useful guidance.

This concluding chapter outlines what are believed to be some of the common features of successful as well as unsuccessful transit strategies introduced for serving suburban markets.

WHAT HAS WORKED?

Relatively successful services can be defined along seven dimensions: (1) Operating environment, (2) Markets, (3) Cost control measures, (4) Vehicle types, (5) Linked services, (6) Small innovations, and (7) Public-private partnerships.

Operating Environment

A distinguishing feature of the more successful suburban transit service strategies has been the servicing of *hubs*—that is, points that represent concentrations of people or of transit vehicles. A *people hub* is a large suburban employment center, like Bishop Ranch in Contra Costa County and the TMC in Houston. A *transit hub* is a designated transit-transfer point, such as that successfully defined and employed by Tidewater Regional Transit (Figure 47) or park-and-ride terminuses operated by Houston METRO. Quite consistently, successful suburban transit services have focused on points where the concentration of activities generates relatively high ridership counts, allows for efficient routing, and eases the transfer process. Some also traverse relatively short routes, which generally allows more frequent passenger turnover per mile logged.

Experiences also suggest that, beyond the hubs themselves, operating along moderately dense suburban corridors is also a likely key to success. For example, all of CCCTA's most cost-effective services operated along relatively dense corridors. Additionally, connecting land-use mixes that consist of all day trip generators is also imperative. CCCTA and Houston METRO, in particular, have carefully aligned suburban routes to connect to medical centers, college campuses, shopping centers, recreational complexes, and community centers, destinations that generate off-peak and weekend trips to complement the peak-hour demands of employment centers.

Collectively, these findings support the long-held belief that compact, mixed-use development is essential toward mounting and sustaining healthy mass transit services. This certainly seems to hold for America's suburbs. These findings lend support to more carefully integrating land-use planning and transit service planning in coming years as a means of strengthening transit's presence in suburbia.

Markets

Some of the more successful suburban services have also served transit's more traditional markets—namely, lower income and working class neighborhoods. Examples are some of CCCTA's more successful crosstown bus routes and the intercounty services linking Riverside, San Bernardino, and Los Angeles counties in southern California. However, there are plenty of good examples of suburban transit successfully serving "choice" customers. Many express shuttles and park-and-ride buses to large-scale employment centers are examples of this.

Cost Control

Some of the more successful suburban services have consciously sought to economize on expenses in numerous ways. One common strategy, often used for DAR and sometimes new shuttle services, is competitive contracting—for example, San Diego Transit, CCCTA, and TRT. Subscription vanpools have also been turned to as a cost-savings strategy. For example, by eliminating wages for drivers, Fort Worth Transit Authority replaced 8 low-productivity fixed-route buses with 12 lower-cost yet higher service quality subscription vans.

Tidewater Regional Transit has been particularly exemplary in introducing suburban service innovations that are effective yet low cost. For example, it uses the entrances of shopping centers and very modest infrastructures as interchange points for its direct transfer centers. Because bus arrivals are so well synchronized, passengers need not spend much time at trans-

Figure 47. Two transfer hubs in suburban Norfolk, Virginia.

fer centers, and there is little pressure to provide posh waiting areas. In fact, during bad weather, customers are invited to stay aboard buses until their connecting buses arrive at the centers. With the Maxi-Ride DAR service, TRT has virtually eliminated expenses for telephone answering, scheduling, and dispatching by shifting these functions to van drivers. Using cellular phones, Maxi-Ride operators function like independent taxi drivers, using their experience and intuition to design services to maximize service quality and satisfy customers.

Vehicle Types

The proper adaption of vehicle fleets to customer demand has also been a hallmark of successful suburban services. Large, comfortable, over-the-road coaches have been essential in attracting choice riders, such as in the case of Houston METRO's crosstown park-and-ride runs. On the other hand, where door-to-door services are provided or shuttles operate within a defined activity center, like a suburban downtown, smaller vans and minibuses have been the vehicles of choice. A particular advantage of small vehicles in more built-up suburban settings is that they tend to generate relatively higher ridership compared with the costs incurred. The advantages of small vehicles include the following: they take less time to load and unload, they arrive more often, they stop less frequently, they are more maneuverable in busy traffic, and they accelerate and decelerate faster. Because of their high load factors, improved performance, and sometimes lower operating costs (because of the typically lower wage rates paid to their drivers), in the right settings, they can provide relatively cost-effective services.

Linked Services

A common characteristic of small-vehicle suburban transit services is that they are linked, providing high interconnectivity. One reason for the success of dial-a-ride and route deviation services, such as San Diego's DART, is that they connect to fixed routes. Dial-a-ride vans operate within a limited territory but efficiently tie to mainline bus routes. This has resulted in a nice blend of flexibly routed services in low-density areas that are tied to lower cost/higher capacity services in built-up areas. Although customers receive less convenient services, the substantial cost savings are widely viewed as more than making up the difference. The case study experiences reviewed in this chapter clearly show that DAR services that link to mainline buses and operate within limited, defined territories are far more cost-effective than more open-ended, nonlinked services.

Linked services have also contributed to the success of many express runs between rail stops and employment centers. The CCCTA bus connections to BART stations and BC Transit's express connections to SkyTrain stations underscore this. Overall, a hierarchy of interconnected services has proven to be among suburban transit's most successful service offerings, with local feeders and circulators complementing a regional structure of mainline routes. The combination of flexible services that operate curb-to-curb, from one's home to a transit center, and mainline connectors that serve major activity centers is one of suburban transit's most cost-effective options.

Service Innovations

Successful suburban service has also creatively adapted transit service practices to the landscape. Where densities are very low, door-to-door services are recognized as the only practical way of competing with the automobile. And where activity centers and concentrated employment areas are spread throughout a service district, timed-transfer hubs have been used as the building blocks for linking these destinations. In this regard, TRT has again been exemplary. The combination of Maxi-Ride DAR and direct transfer center services has produced a hybrid form of mass transit that is well suited to cost-effectively serving the region's spread-out landscape and, consequently, the predominant many-to-many pattern of travel. San Diego's linkage of dial-a-ride vans, mainline buses, express buses, and trolley stops also represents a successful adaption of transit service types to the lay of the land.

Public-Private Cosponsorship

Because of the inherent risks involved in mounting suburban transit services, the greatest inroads in establishing service innovations have been made when both the public and private sectors work together. Successful express runs between suburban employment centers and rail stops or park-and-ride lots have been cosponsored by employers and transit agencies in Contra Costa County, Houston, and San Diego. Developers have helped finance services, such as the noontime shuttles serving Bishop Ranch.

WHAT HASN'T WORKED?

Of course, with the good comes the bad. Just as there have been successful examples of suburban transit services in the United States, the 11 case studies also clearly point to a number of failures. General public DAR services that are not linked and that are not confined to a zone have consistently resulted in extremely high per rider deficits, often on the order of $10 or more per passenger trip. Midday shuttles targeted at suburban employment centers have also been unable to attract substantial legions of loyal customers. Several edge cities in Houston eliminated these services because of the inordinately high deficits incurred. Part of the problem is thought to be the prevalence of free parking in many of these places. Cheap parking encourages solo commuting, thus substantially reducing the demand for midday mobility to off-site restaurants and shops.

Experiences with operating specialized, crosstown shuttles between low-income neighborhoods and suburban job sites have also generally been unsuccessful. Portland's Tri-Met incurred very high deficits in connecting residents of low-income, Enterprise Zone communities to suburban job sites, as has the Fort Worth Transportation Authority. In many cases, the problems seems to be that the residents of these areas were unqualified for job opportunities at the serviced employment sites. These experiences speak to the reality that the challenges of reducing joblessness lie far beyond connecting residents to job centers via transit.

Lastly, the rapid growth in suburban employment has given rise to a tremendous growth in crosstown, circumferential trip making over the past decade. The only attempt to serve such demand through introducing circumferential bus services, at least among the case sites reviewed, has incurred extremely high deficits. Notably, Houston's TC Flyer, which circulates along Houston's I-610 beltloop, has incurred deficits of nearly $23 per passenger trip in 1995. This is partly because buses operate on intensive 15-min headways. This was viewed as necessary to provide a service that is time competitive with the private automobile. Because the opportunities for circumferential bus services are probably better in Houston than anywhere (given its large number of edge cities, HOV lanes, and cobweb-like freeway network), there is probably little likelihood that such services will meet with success any time in the near future.

WHERE TO GO FROM HERE: FUTURE DIRECTIONS

A common problem encountered in planning new suburban services is limited resources—both time and money. In the case of DART's planning for suburban services, staff were unable to concentrate their efforts on optimizing services; rather, the emphasis was on fast implementation. This has sometimes been a result of public pressure to quickly mount services to respond to rapid rates of growth. Extensive public involvement has also in instances led to transit agencies being overly ambitious in supplying new services, resulting in escalating deficits.

Because the suburban transit industry is still largely in its infancy and much remains to be learned, it is essential that future service planning embody some degree of experimentation. If we are to push the boundaries of innovative and adaptive suburban transit services, then pilot programs of new, largely untried service strategies, like private jitney feeders to suburban mainline bus routes or crosstown door-to-door shuttle vans akin to airport shuttles, will be needed. Because of the inherent risks involved in mounting innovative pilot programs, it is likely that some degree of cost sharing between different levels of government as well as both the public and private sectors will be necessary if creative, new forms of suburban transit services are to be tried.

Accompanying experimentation should be more comprehensive service monitoring and evaluation programs. Because of budget and time constraints, evaluation has all too often been an afterthought. To properly assess impacts and control for potential confounding influences, it is essential that a rich, longitudinal database, with both before and after data points, be compiled over time. Indeed, a serious limitation to conducting this research was the absence of suitable data and statistical controls to allow suburban service strategies to be carefully evaluated.

Several of the service strategies found among case studies were products of pilot demonstration programs. LANTA experimented with general public dial-a-ride services in response to growing demands for services to shopping malls and entertainment centers on weekends. During the pilot, minor adjustments were made in routing and scheduling, leading to the establishment of permanent weekend and off-peak mall shuttle leads. Experiences show that new service innovations require time, normally 1 to 2 years, to mature and for markets to develop. Thus, a certain amount of patience must go along with experimentation and risk taking.

This research shows that comprehensive evaluations of suburban transit services will have to wait a number of years until considerably more service strategies have been introduced across more places that have had sufficient time to evolve. More transit operators can be expected to introduce new and unique transit services that are specially targeted to suburban markets in years to come. To properly evaluate these programs, however, it is essential that considerable resources be given to the tasks of project monitoring and evaluation. In particular, sufficient data over a number of time points need to be compiled to allow the influences of new services to be distinguished from the effects of other potential explanatory factors. It was the absence of rich longitudinal data and control variables that limited the researchers' ability to thoroughly evaluate the performance of different service strategies.

BIBLIOGRAPHY

Atlanta Regional Commission, *Transportation Problems and Strategies for Major Activity Centers in the Atlanta Region,* Atlanta (1985).

American Public Transit Association, *APTA Fact Book: 1994–1995,* Washington, D.C. (1995).

Arndt, J. *Private/Public Partnerships to Serve Suburban Markets,* Metropolitan Transit Authority, Houston, Tex. (May 1995).

Arrington, G.B., *Beyond the Field of Dreams: Light Rail and Growth Management in Portland,* Tri-Met, Portland, Ore. (1995).

Baerwald, T., "Land Use Change in Suburban Clusters and Corridors," *Transportation Research Record 861,* Transportation Research Board, Washington, D.C. (1982) pp. 7–12.

Balloffett and Associates, Inc., *RTD Strategic Plan: Peer City Review, Technical Memorandum 4* (1993).

BC Transit, *Maple Ridge and Pitt Meadows Service Review* (November 1992).

BC Transit, *1995/96 Annual Service Plan* (December 1992).

BC Transit, *Vancouver Region 10-Year Bus Development Plan* (no date given).

BC Transit, *Transit and Nodal Development* (October 1991).

Behnke, R., *German "Smart Bus" Systems: Potential Applications in Portland, Oregon,* Federal Transit Administration, U.S. Department of Transportation, Washington, D.C. (1993).

Bernick, M. and Cervero, R. *Transit Villages in the 21st Century,* McGraw-Hill, New York (1996).

Bernick, M. and Cervero, R., "Transit-Based Development in the United States," *Passenger Transport,* Vol. 12, No. 2, (1994) pp. 7–8.

Bonetti, E., "UNC's Shuttle Service: A Role Model." *The Parking Professional* (November 1994).

Booz-Allen & Hamilton Inc. et al., *San Diego County System Strategic Plan* (November 1993).

Calthorpe, P., *The Next American Metropolis,* Princeton University Architectural Press, Princeton, N.J. (1994).

Cambridge Systematics, *TCRP J-6 Transit Ridership Initiative,* Transit Cooperative Research Program, Transportation Research Board, Washington, D.C. (August 1994).

Campbell, J., "Increasing Transit's Share of the Metropolitan Travel Market." *Innovation Briefs* (1994).

Cervero, R., *Suburban Gridlock,* Center for Urban Policy Research, New Brunswick (1986).

Cervero, R., "Jobs-Housing Balancing and Regional Mobility." *Journal of the American Planning Association,* Vol. 55, No. 2 (1989) pp. 136–150.

Cervero, R., *Ridership Impacts of Transit-Focused Development in California,* Monograph 54. Institute of Urban and Regional Development, Berkeley (1993).

Cervero, R. and Landis, J., "Suburbanization of Jobs and the Journey to Work: A Submarket Analysis of Commuting in the San Francisco Bay Area." *Journal of Advanced Transportation,* Vol. 26, No. 3 (1992) pp. 275–297.

Cervero, R. and Dunzo, M., *An Assessment of Suburban-Targeted Transit Service Strategies in the United States,* Research Report 145. University of California Transportation Center, Berkeley (1993).

Cervero, R. and Menotti, V., *Market Profiles of Rail-Based Housing Projects in California,* Working Paper 622. Institute of Urban and Regional Development, Berkeley (1994).

Cervero, R., "Surviving in the Suburbs: Transit's Untapped Frontier." *Access,* Vol. 2 (1993) pp. 29–34.

Cervero, R., *America's Suburban Centers: The Land Use-Transportation Link,* Unwin-Hyman, Boston (1989).

Cervero, R., *Ridership Impacts of Transit-Focussed Development in California,* Monograph 45. Institute of Urban and Regional Development, Berkeley (1993).

Cervero, R., *Transit-Supportive Development in the United States: Experiences and Prospects,* Federal Transit Administration, U.S. DOT, Washington, D.C. (1994).

Cervero, R., "Making Transit Work in the Suburbs." *Transportation Research Record 1451,* Transportation Research Board, Washington, D.C. (1994) pp. 3–11.

Cervero, R., *Paratransit in America: Redefining Mass Transportation,* Praeger Press, Westport, Conn. (1995).

Chinitz, B., *Metropolitan America in Transition: Implications for Land Use and Transportation Planning: Summary of Proceedings,* Lincoln Land Institute, Federal Highway Administration, and Federal Transit Administration, Arlington, Va. (1993).

COMSIS Corporation, *Overview of Travel Demand Management Measures,* Federal Highway Administration, U.S. Department of Transportation, Washington, D.C. (1994).

Corporation of the District of Burnaby, *Metrotown: A Time and a Place* (December 1992).

Dallas Area Rapid Transit, *FY 1996 Financial Plan* (November 1995).

Dallas Area Rapid Transit, *Transit System Plan* (November 1995).

Dallas Area Rapid Transit, *DART Service Standards* (September 1995).

Dallas Area Rapid Transit, *DART: A Progress Report* (Summer 1995).

Dallas Area Rapid Transit, *1993 Annual Report: The Tie That Binds* (1993).

Davis, B., "Car Use: Lifeblood May Turn to Poison." *The Edge City News,* Vol. 3, No. 1, (1995) pp. 1–3.

Davis, B., Ed., *The Edge City News,* Vol. 1, No. 9, Warrenton, Va. (February 1994).

Douglass, B., *Comparison of Commuting Trends Between Downtown, Suburban Centers, and Suburban Campuses in the Washington Metropolitan Area,* Parsons-Brinckerhoff-Tudor-Bechtel, Inc., Washington, D. C. (1992).

"Special Edition: The Future of Getting People Around." *Edge City News,* Vol. 1, No. 9, Broad Run, Va. (February 1994).

Ewing, R., Haliyur, P., and Page, G., "Getting Around a Traditional City, a Suburban PUD and Everything In-Between." *Alternative Transportation: Planning, Design, Issues, Solutions: Proceedings of the Fourteenth International Pedestrian Conference,* Go Boulder, Boulder, Colo. (1993) pp. 21–30.

Faux, P., "Edge Cities are the Choice of Small Firms." *The Edge City News 2*, Vol. 6 (1994) p. 7.

Fish, C., Dock, F., and Baltutis, W., *Lake-Cook Corridor Suburb-to-Suburb Commuter Demonstration Project*, paper presented at the 74th Annual Transportation Research Board Meeting (January 1995).

Fulks, T., "A California TMA Entices Local Organizations to Lend Passengers Vans for Transit Use." *TMA Clearinghouse Quarterly*, Vol. 3, No. 1 (Winter 1994).

Garreau, J., *Edge City: Life on the Frontier*, Viking, New York (1991).

Giuliano, G. and Small, K., "Subcenters in the Los Angeles Region." *Regional Science and Urban Economics*, Vol. 5 (1991) pp. 305–312.

Giuliano, G. and Small, K., "Is the Journey to Work Explained by Urban Structure?" *Urban Studies*, Vol. 30, No. 9 (1993) pp. 1485–1500.

Giuliano, G. and R. Teal, *Privately Provided Commuter Bus Services: Experiences, Problems, and Prospects, Urban Transit: The Private Challenge to Public Transportation*, C. Lave, ed., Ballinger, Cambridge, Mass. (1985).

Gordon, P., Richardson, H., and Wong, H., "The Distribution of Population and Employment in a Polycentric City: The Case of Los Angeles." *Environment and Planning*, Vol. 18 (1986) pp. 161–173.

Greater Vancouver Regional District, *Livable Region Strategic Plan* (October 1995).

Grzesiakowski, T., "PACE's Experiences with Sears's Move to Hoffman Estates," *Proceedings of the Second Annual Metropolitan Conference on Public Transportation Research*, Chicago (1993).

"HART and Westshore Alliance Begin Shuttle Service." *Passenger Transport* (December 5, 1994).

Hartshorn, T. and Muller, P., *Suburban Business Centers: Employment Implications*, Economic Development Administration, Washington, D. C. (1986).

Hanley, R., "A New Kind of Suburbia Arises out of the New Jersey Farmlands." *New York Times* (July 3, 1995).

Heikkila, E., Gordon, P., Kim, J., Peiser, R., Richardson, H., and Dale-Johnson, D., "What Happened to the CBD-Distance Gradient?" *Environment and Planning*, Vol. 21 (1989) pp. 221–232.

Hooper, K., "Travel Characteristics of Large-Scale Suburban Activity Centers," *NCHRP Report 323*, Transportation Research Board, Washington, D. C. (1989).

Hooper, K., *Access to Opportunity*, American Public Transit Association, Washington, D. C. (May 1994).

Houston Area Research Council, *Major Activity Centers in the United States*, Houston Area Research Council, Center for Growth Studies, Houston, Tex. (1989).

Hufstedler, G., *DART's Transit Center Based System: Successes and Failures in Low Density Suburbs*, Presented at the APTA Bus Operations and Technology Conference (May 1994).

Hughes, M., *Regional Economics and Edge Cities, Edge City and ISTEA: Examining the Transportation Implications of Suburban Development Patterns*, Federal Transit Administration, U.S. DOT, Washington, D. C. (1992).

Hurwitz, E. "San Diego's Strong Public-Private Partnership." *Transit California* (February 1996).

Jarzeb, J., *Suburban Transit: Diversity in the Land of the Niche Market*, paper presentation, APTA Bus Operations Conference, Reno, Nev. (May 1995).

Joint Planning Commission Lehigh-Northampton Counties, *Community Planning and Transit: A Case for Transit Supportive Design* (April 1995).

Joint Planning Commission Lehigh-Northampton Counties, *Lehigh and Northampton Transportation Authority: LANTA/Whitehall Township Transit Survey* (March 1994).

Joint Planning Commission Lehigh-Northampton Counties, *Lehigh Valley Profile and Trends* (May 1995).

Joint Planning Commission Lehigh-Northampton Counties, *Transportation System Evaluation: 1995 Update* (June 1995).

Lehigh and Northampton Transportation Authority, *Public Transportation: An Essential Investment*, White Paper on the Importance of Public Transportation in the Lehigh Valley (February 1995).

Lehigh and Northampton Transportation Authority, *Strategic Plan, 1993–2003: Taking Public Transit into the 21st Century* (January 1993).

Leinberger, C., *Suburbia. Land Use in Transition: Emerging Forces and Issues Shaping the Real Estate Environment*, The Urban Land Institute, Washington, D.C. (1993) pp. 62–71.

Long Island Regional Planning Board, *The Journey to Work to Major Employment Centers*, Long Island Regional Planning Board, Hauppauge, N.Y. (1994).

Maloney, L., "America's Suburbs Still Alive and Doing Fine." *U.S. News and World Report* (March 12, 1984).

Margolis, J., *Municipal Fiscal Structure in a Metropolitan Region*, Urban Economics: Readings and Analysis, R. Grieson, ed., Little Brown, Boston (1973).

Maryland National Capital Park and Planning Commission, *Suburban Activity Centers in the Washington Area*, National Capital Park and Planning Commission, Silver Spring, Md. (1990).

"MBTA Opens Crosstown Routes," *Passenger Transport* (September 26, 1994).

METRO, *METRO: Action for a Cleaner Tomorrow* (January 1994).

METRO, *The Transit Services Program: Fiscal Years 1995–1999*.

METRO, *The Transit Services Program: Fiscal Years 1996–2000*.

METRO, *The 292 Westwood/TNC Park-and-Ride Follow-up Research* (June 1995).

METRO, *METRO Facts* (1995).

Metropolitan Transit Development Board, *Metropolitan San Diego Short Range Transit Plan: FY 1995–2001* (June 1994).

Metropolitan Transit Development Board, *Nontransit Funding of New Bus Services, Policies and Procedures No. 40* (September 1990).

Metropolitan Transit Development Board, *Providing Transit Services, Policies and Procedures No. 32* (February 1993).

Metropolitan Transit Development Board, *Short Range Transit Plan Update: FY 1996–2003* (August 1995).

Metropolitan Transportation Commission, *Transit Vouchers Top Quarter Million Mark*, Oakland, Calif. (January 18, 1995).

Middleton, W., "How Denver's Eco Pass Encourages Transit Use." *Transit Connections* (March 1995).

Minerva, V., Sampson, D., and Levinson, H., *Employer Shuttles—Concepts and Case Studies*, the 75th Annual Transportation Research Board Meeting (January 1996).

Montgomery County Ride-On, *Serving Neighborhoods: Feeder and Fixed Schedule, Variable Route Service*, Montgomery Co., MD (1995).

Muller, P., *Transportation and Urban Form: Stages in the Spatial Evolution of the American Metropolis*, The Geography of Urban Transportation, Guilford Press, New York (1981) pp. 24–48.

Multisystems, Inc., *Paratransit for the Work Trip: Commuter Ridesharing,* Urban Mass Transportation Administration, U.S. DOT, Washington, D.C. (1982).

Nelessen, A. and Howe, L., *Flexible Friendly Neighborhood Transit: A Solution for the Suburban Transportation Dilemma* (no date given).

New Jersey Transit Corporation, *CMAQ Funded Wheels Experimental Services Minibus Ridership Recap* (January 1995).

New Jersey Transit Corporation, *CMAQ Funded Wheels Experimental Services Minibus Ridership Recap* (September 1996).

Newman, P. and Kenworthy, J., "Gasoline Consumption and Cities: A Comparison of U.S. Cities with a Global Survey." *Journal of the American Planning Association,* Vol. 55, No. 1 (1989) pp. 24–37.

PACE, *PACE Development Guidelines,* Chicago, Ill. (December 1989).

Parks, R., *Transit and the "Unchained Metropolis": Using a Transit-Center Based System to Penetrate the Evolving Suburban-to-Suburban Travel Market* (undated).

Phillips, D., "Transit Equity: Tackling the 'City vs. Suburb' Issue." *Transit Connections* (June 1995).

"Pioneer Valley Implementing New Routes," *Passenger Transport,* (September 26, 1994).

Pisarski, A., *New Perspectives in Commuting,* Federal Highway Administration, U.S. DOT, Washington, D.C. (July 1992).

Pisarski, A., *Travel Behavior Issues in the 1990s,* Federal Highway Administration, U.S. DOT, Washington, D.C.

Pisarski, A., *New Perspectives on Commuting,* Federal Highway Administration, U.S. DOT, Washington, D.C. (1992).

Pivo, G., "The Net of Mixed Beads: Suburban Office Development in Six Metropolitan Areas." *Journal of the American Planning Association,* Vol. 56, No. 4 (1990) pp. 457–469.

Purvis, C., *County-to-County Commute Patterns in the San Francisco Bay Area,* Working Paper 3, Metropolitan Transportation Commission, Oakland, Calif. (1992).

Pushkarev, B. and Zupan, J., *Public Transportation and Land Use Policy,* University Press, Bloomington, Ind. (1977).

Rice Center for Urban Mobility Research, *Houston's Major Activity Centers and Worker Travel Behavior,* Houston-Galveston Area Council (1987).

Riverside Transit Agency, *RTA NTD Report for FY 1995 (Section 15)* (October 1995).

Riverside Transit Agency, *Western Riverside County Long Range Transit Working Paper* (February 1994).

Riverside Transit Agency, *Riverside Transit Agency Short Range Transit Plan FY 1995–2001.*

Riverside Transit Agency, *Build the Vision,* RTA Board of Directors Retreat Packet (March 1995).

Sacramento Regional Transit District, *Design Guidelines for Bus and Light Rail Facilities* (no date given).

Sampson, D., *Assessing the Impact of Rail to Work Shuttles for Suburban Employment Centers,* APTA Bus Operations Conference, Richmond, Va. (1994)

San Diego Association of Governments, "A Look at San Diego's Future: The Series 8 Regionwide Forecast 1990–2015." *INFO* (January/February 1994).

San Diego Association of Governments, *Land Use Elements of the Regional Growth Managment Strategy* (Autumn 1995).

San Diego Association of Governments, "Profiling the Region's Major Statistical Areas." *INFO* (May/June 1995).

San Diego Association of Governments, "Regional Activity Centers." *INFO* (March/April 1995).

San Diego Association of Governments, "Regional Employment Inventory." *INFO* (March/April 1994).

Savas, E., and Cantarella, A., *A Comparative Study of Public and Private Bus Operations in New York City,* Federal Transit Administration, U.S. DOT, Washington, D.C. (1992).

Schneider, J., *Transit and the Polycentric City,* U.S. DOT, Urban Mass Transportation Administration, Washington, D.C. (1981).

Smerk, G., "Structuring Regional Transit: One Size Does Not Fit All." *Transit Connections* (March 1995).

Snohomish County Transportation Authority, *A Guide to Land Use and Public Transportation,* U.S. DOT, Washington, D.C. (December 1989).

Song, S., *Monocentric and Polycentric Density Functions and Their Required Commutes,* Working Paper 198, The University of California Transportation Center, Berkeley (1992).

South Central Regional Council of Governments, *Union Station-Downtown Transit Study—Current Transit Service,* Memorandum for the Union Station Downtown Waterfront Links Study (September 1994).

Speare, A., *Changes in Urban Growth Patterns 1980–90,* Lincoln Institute of Land Policy, Cambridge, Mass. (1993).

Stanback, T., *The New Suburbanization: Challenge to the Central City,* Westview Press, Boulder, Colo. (1991).

Stone, J., *Winston-Salem Mobility Management: An Example of APTS Benefits,* North Carolina State University, Civil Engineering Program, Raleigh (1995).

Transit California, *RTA: Community Involvement Supporting Quality Customer Service* (January 1996).

Tri-County Metropolitan Transportation District of Oregon, *Planning and Design for Transit,* Portland, Ore. (March 1993).

Tidewater Regional Transit, *TRT On-Board Ridership Survey* (1992).

Urban Land Institute, *Land Use in Transition: Emerging Forces and Issues Shaping the Real Estate Environment,* The Urban Land Institute, Washington, D.C. (1993).

Urban Mobility Corporation, *The White Flint Shuttle: A Negotiated Trip Reduction Initiative,* Private Sector Briefs, Washington, D.C. (July 1992).

Urban Mobility Corporation, *Houston: Competitive Contracting Update,* Private Sector Briefs, Washington, D.C. (March 1993).

Urban Mobility Corporation, *Residential-Based Transportation Services,* Private Sector Briefs, Washington, D.C. (May 1993).

Urban Mobility Corporation, *Congestion Management in Montgomery County, MD,* Innovation Briefs, Washington, D.C. (June 1994).

Urban Mobility Corporation, *Transit Villages,* Innovation Briefs, Washington, D.C. (February 1995).

Urban Mobility Corporation, *Livable Communities: Lessons from Abroad,* Innovation Briefs, Washington, D.C. (August 1995).

Urban Mass Transportation Administration, *Small City Transit: El Cajon, California: Citywide Shared-Ride Taxi Service,* U.S. DOT, Washington, D.C. (1976).

Urbitran Associates, Inc., *South Wilton Commuter Connection Feasibility Study,* South Western Regional Planning Agency (January 1994).

Urbitran Associates, Inc., *Union Station Downtown New Haven Waterfront Links Study,* South Central Regional Council of Governments (May 1995).

Urbitran Associates, Inc., *Stamford Shuttle Feasibility Study,* The Stamford Partnership (1986).

Urbitran Associates, Inc., *Suburban Initiatives Project Feasibility Studies (10 Study Areas),* New Jersey Transit Corporation (1993).

Vance, J., *The Scene of Man: The Role and Structure of the City in the Geography of Western Civilization,* Harper's College Press, New York (1977).

APPENDIX A

CLASSIFYING SUBURBAN ENVIRONMENTS

DEFINING SUBURBAN ENVIRONMENTS

It has been observed that America's suburbs are a kaleidoscope of activities. Indeed, many of today's suburbs are as diverse and varied as traditional downtowns and urban centers. Residential neighborhoods can range from master-planned, walled-in subdivisions with one-quarter-acre estates to midrise apartments clustered around rail stations, such as in Ballston, Virginia, and Pleasant Hill, California. Today's job sites vary from campuses with generous landscaping and open spaces dotted with single-story structures to edge cities, like Houston's Post Oak and Bellevue, Washington, where shiny 30-story office towers stretch skyward, intermixed with retail shops, hotels, and apartment complexes. The activities found at some suburban centers read like inventories of traditional downtown facilities—corporate headquarters, five-star hotels, boutiques, specialty shops, convention halls, and government offices. Increasingly, major trip generators such as airports, recreational theme parks, sports stadia, cultural centers, and megamalls are also locating along the metropolitan fringes.

An important task in this project is to define the kinds of suburban environments that mass transportation systems operate in throughout suburban America. Such a topology will allow different service delivery strategies, pricing programs, and institutional arrangements that are best suited to different suburban operating and market environments to be more clearly defined and evaluated and a representative set of case studies to be selected. The purpose of this appendix is to develop this topology. It summarizes the text of the Task 2 report, which was submitted as a free-standing document in June 1995. References in this appendix are found in the *Bibliography*.

The first task in defining suburban environments is to try to define the term "suburb." The distinction between what is "suburban" and what is "urban" has blurred in recent times. A clinical definition of the suburbs, used by the U.S. Bureau of the Census, is the geographic portion of a metropolitan statistical area (MSA) that lies outside the MSA's central city or cities. This generally means that political boundaries distinguish suburbs from central cities, even though activities on both sides of the boundary may be virtually identical.

In general, suburbs have been associated with low-density and often relatively new development. Densities typically decline as one moves farther out toward the metropolitan periphery. Among the landmarks of suburbia are single-family detached homes, indoor shopping malls and open-air retail plazas, strip commercial development, sprawling business and industrial parks, and generous amounts of open space and public parkland. Socioeconomically, suburbanites tend to be better off than their central city counterparts. And ethnically, suburbs tend to be more homogenous, historically dominated by white, middle-class households. Increasingly, however, even these generalizations become difficult. In most metropolitan areas, one can find suburbs that are new and old, that are affluent and working class in character, and that are predominantly white and of mixed races. *The point being made here is that suburbs are not just statistical or political artifacts but rather meaningful sociological and cultural entities that often defy precise definition.*

From a physical standpoint, suburbia is often used interchangeably with such terms as "sprawl" and "scatteration." Perhaps foremost these terms conjure images of a very low-density, spread-out settlement pattern. Some, however, might argue there is little inherent pattern in suburban sprawl. Such terms often carry with them a pejorative, almost amorphous connotation.

One form of suburban development that has stood out from the somewhat vague notion of a sprawling suburban landscape has been concentrated mixed-use development, what we generically call "suburban centers." Over the past 20 years, many U.S. metropolitan areas have witnessed the emergence of distinct activity centers, both in central cities and in the suburbs, each with its own catchment or zone of influence (Vance, 1977; Muller, 1981). More popular accounts of minicities that have sprouted along the metropolitan periphery since the 1970s, such as Garreau's *Edge City* (1991), have raised the national consciousness about this new form of suburbia. A common characteristic of all suburban centers is their large daytime workforce. To a large degree, America's suburban centers owe their existence to the rapid pace of employment decentralization over the past 20 years (Cervero, 1989). Some suburban employment centers are on the metropolitan fringes and have distinct suburban characters (e.g., shiny new buildings, strict zoning codes, nearby large-lot residential subdivisions), whereas others are in more mature, inner-tier areas. Perimeter Center (a large office complex and regional shopping center north of Atlanta) is an example of the former and Bethesda's cluster of offices around its Washington Metrorail station represents more of the latter. Still other concentrations of suburban development function more as satellites, straddled between two or more central cites. The Research Triangle, for instance, lies approximately 15 mi (24 km) west of Raleigh,

North Carolina, and operates more as a satellite employment center than as a suburb of the Raleigh-Durham-Chapel Hill metropolitan area. Perhaps the feature that these centers have most in common is that they are "non-central business district" or "non-CBD" locales.

In this light, this study adopts a definition of suburbia as places that lie outside of CBDs and central cities, generally with population densities below 2,000 persons per square mile and with floor area ratios below 1.0. This definition is used loosely, however, and is meant to convey a low-density area outside a traditional urban center.

CLASSIFYING SUBURBS BY LAND-USE ENVIRONMENT

Suburban environments can be defined along multiple dimensions. For this project, the researchers propose classifying suburban environments mainly in terms of their physical land-use characteristics, mainly on the grounds that travel choices and transit service types are highly correlated with factors such as density and land-use composition.

America's suburbs have experienced three waves of growth in terms of their land-use environments. The first wave consisted largely of residential growth, with millions of working class and middle-to-upper-income households leaving cities throughout the past century in search of detached single-family homes and more spacious living conditions. Bedroom communities like Levittown in Long Island and Mission Viejo in Southern California epitomize this first wave of mass suburban development. The second wave involved retail businesses migrating outward closer to their customer base, locating along commercial strips, in regional shopping malls, and in everything in between. The "malling of America" marked an era where retail sales fell sharply in the downtowns of many small- and medium-sized cities. With the rapid decentralization of jobs in the 1980s, America entered into its third wave of suburbanization. The exodus of jobs has meant that many suburbs have come full circle, featuring the same activities found in traditional cities, though often spread over a much larger geographic area. This has meant that more and more Americans are living, shopping, and working in lower density settings that are less and less conducive to transit riding.

America's suburbs can be classified by the land uses that dominated during these three waves of growth. In the hierarchy for this project, suburban land-use environments are distinguished in terms of the degree to which residential, commercial-retail, and office-employment uses predominate.

RESIDENTIAL SUBURBS

Residential development remains the dominant land use in America's suburbs, and the suburbs continue to capture the bulk of population growth. In 1990, over one-half of the nation's population lived in the 39 metropolitan areas containing over one million residents (Hughes, 1992). The suburban population in these areas increased 55 percent between 1970 and 1990, whereas the traditional, central city population increased only 2 percent.

In every metropolitan area of the United States, suburban enclaves that almost exclusively consist of residential housing can be found. These bedroom communities export their resident-workers to jobs elsewhere in the region, thus representing the origins of commute trips in the morning and destinations during evening hours. Margolis (1973) referred to bedroom communities as suburbs with ratios of jobs-to-employed residents below 0.80. For example, by this definition, 3 of the 18 largest suburban communities in the San Francisco Bay Area in 1990 were bedroom communities, with ratios of jobs-to-employed residents in parentheses: Daly City (0.44), Fremont (0.76), and Vallejo (0.79).

Perhaps the factor that best distinguishes predominantly residential suburbs is their housing stock and relative densities. In this study, residential suburbs are distinguished as predominantly single-family or mixed housing (single-family, apartments, other housing).

This two-part distinction most directly reflects differences in residential densities. Indirectly, it captures income differentials in suburbia (i.e., typically younger, lower-income households occupy mixed-housing environments). Mixed-housing environments, for example, are likely to be denser with more captive ridership markets, perhaps providing a suburban setting where transit has a greater chance of competing with the private automobile.

Forecasters call for a healthy recovery in the suburban single-family home market in the mid-to-late 1990s (Leinberger, 1993). The major reason for this is the pent-up demand for home ownership among baby boomers, the youngest of whom are in their early 30s and entering a time of their lives when people move up to larger homes. With many new jobs locating on the extreme edges of metropolitan areas, there will be pressures over the next 5 years for future single-family housing developments on what is now rural land 20 to 25 mi (32 to 40 km) beyond newly emerging job centers like Plano (Dallas), Scottsdale (Phoenix), Redmond (Seattle), and Alpharetta (Atlanta).

In terms of multifamily rental housing, the bulk of projects built in the 1980s stand along major inner suburban corridors in low-density configurations (12 to 18 units to the acre, in two-story walkups). Forecasters predict that much of apartment and condominium construction in the mid-to-late 1990s will be in the new outer suburbs, near emerging edge cities (e.g., Gainesville in northern Virginia and Peachtree City outside Atlanta) or immediately adjacent to existing inner-ring edge cities (e.g., Ballston, Virginia, and Atlanta's Buckhead district).

Another emerging market niche of multifamily development is rail-based housing projects. Nationwide, around 12,000 apartment and condominium units were built within a one-quarter-mi (0.4-km) ring of rail stations across 10 different metropolitan areas from 1988 to 1993, with nearly 500 units built on land owned by transit authorities (Bernick and Cervero, 1994). In the San Francisco Bay Area alone, 11 multifamily projects containing over 4,500 units were built within a one-quarter-mi radius of a Bay Area rail station between 1988 and 1993.

COMMERCIAL AND MIXED-USE SUBURBS

Retail activities generally follow a central-place hierarchy, with small outlets and retail plazas (under 20,000 ft^2) serving neighborhoods, larger shopping centers (under 200,000 ft^2) serving communities, and still larger shopping malls (above 200,000 ft^2) serving regions and subregions. What all these settings have in common is a strong automobile orientation—underscored by large asphalt surface parking lots, wide connecting boulevards, and sprawling structures. Contemporary shopping centers are perhaps the least friendly environments for transit or pedestrian access anywhere. Often bus riders are dropped off at the periphery of parking lots, forced to walk long distances through a sea of parking to reach stores. The perimeters of many suburban shopping malls do not even have sidewalks. Except for those too young, old, or poor to own and drive a car, bus transit is largely ignored as a serious travel option by suburban shoppers. A recent survey of shoppers at two suburban malls in the Bay Area, for instance, found that fewer than 3 percent reached the malls by transit (Cervero, 1993).

With the tremendous growth in discount-warehouse retailers in recent years, if anything the automobile orientation of retail establishments in the United States has increased in recent times. Big-box retail outlets like Home Depot, Blockbuster Video, Circuit City, and Price Costco have redefined the suburban retail market, relying on high-volume sales of durable goods and consumer items sold at wholesale discounts to lure shoppers away from malls. Many big-box outlets are sited as stand-alone structures or in "power centers" in peripheral locations where land is cheap and automobile access is necessary. The "build it and they will come" philosophy often prevails in the siting of large warehouse retailers.

According to forecasts from the Urban Land Institute (1993), the major growth segment in retailing will be the community-based power center—typically 250,000 to 500,000 ft^2 (23,226 to 46,451 km^2), occupied by two or more large discount chains, with a small amount of remaining floorspace leased to small tenants. Growth in other retail segments will likely be slower. Activities in the regional mall market will split between the construction of new malls on the suburban-exurban fringes and renovation of existing inner suburban malls, including construction of outlets on existing parking lots (as inner-tier suburban centers continue to densify) (Leinberger, 1993). Observers also forecast a continued expansion of neighborhood retailers in suburbia, mainly involving restaurants, convenience stores, and drug stores that are oriented toward residential development. Still, shopping malls and neighborhood outlets are threatened by the steady expansion of national chains and warehouse retailers, so their long-term prognosis remains unclear.

Because suburban retail environments have never been a natural habitat for mass transit services and probably never will be, little would be gained in conducting case studies under TCRP Project B-6 for different classes of retail environments. The researchers believe that a better classification of suburban communities is the degree to which they are balanced in terms of jobs and housing. Balanced communities feature a mix of housing, population-serving retail, private companies, and business-serving retail. Thus, in contrast to bedroom communities and employment centers, balanced communities maintain comparable numbers of jobs and employed residents. According to Margolis (1973) and Cervero (1989), balanced communities average ratios of jobs to employed-residents in the range 0.80 to 1.20. In 1990, one-half of the Bay Area's largest suburban communities—9 of 18—had ratios in this range; they were Alameda, Concord, Napa, San Mateo, Richmond, Fairfield, Mountain View, Redwood City, and Pleasanton.

In summary, a third suburban land-use classification used in this research is balanced, mixed-use suburb. In all balanced, mixed suburbs, retail activities are prominent land uses, as are residential housing and employment concentrations.

SUBURBAN EMPLOYMENT CENTERS AND CLUSTERS

The most pronounced change that has taken place in America's suburban landscape over the past two decades has been the emergence of large-scale employment centers. The movement of jobs from the metropolitan core to the metropolitan periphery has been spurred by postindustrialization—the restructuring of America's economy from a predominantly manufacturing base to a service and information-processing orientation. Factors such as availability of cheaper land, easier access to labor, lower taxes, improved telecommunication links, and closer proximity to regional airports have spurred this exodus (Cervero, 1989). Although many decentralizing jobs have involved back-office support functions, increasingly corporate headquarters and entire companies in fields like finance, retailing, and wholesaling are relocating to the suburbs and exurbs (Stanback, 1991; Leinberger, 1993).

The New York metropolitan area mirrors the spatial changes that took place in many large U.S. regions during the 1980s. From 1980 to 1990, Manhattan added 54 million ft^2 (5 million m^2) of office space; the suburban ring, including Long Island, northeastern New Jersey, and Westchester County, added 173 million ft^2 (16 million m^2) (equal to the entire Chicago metropolitan office market) (Hughes, 1992). Thus, suburban counties captured two-thirds of the region's office growth during the 1980s. Overall, Manhattan still accounted for 56 percent of all office space in the region, but its market share fell from 85 percent.

SUBCENTERING AND POLYCENTRIC GROWTH

Because of job decentralization, the spatial structures of most U.S. metropolitan areas have changed noticeably from a single-centered to a multicentered, or polycentric, form over the past two decades. A number of empirical studies have documented the emergence of subcenters in the United States. Using minimum thresholds related to employment densities and size (or floorspace), analysts have identified 13 subcenters in greater Washington, D.C. (Garreau, 1991), 17 in greater Atlanta (Atlanta Regional Commission, 1985), and 22 in the Houston-Galveston area (Rice Center for Urban Mobility, 1987). Four separate studies of the Los Angeles region have identified between 6 and 54 subcenters there (Gordon et al., 1986; Heikkila et al., 1989; Giuliano and Small, 1991; Song, 1992). More recently, Speare (1994) counted 188 central places in greater Los Angeles, 65 in metropolitan Detroit, and 39 in the Houston-Galveston region. These centers have proven difficult to label, giving rise to a variety of names like "suburban downtowns," "edge cities," "subcities," and "technopolises" (Hartshorne and Muller, 1986; Scott and Angel, 1987; Cervero, 1989; Garreau, 1991).

Statistically, the distinguishing feature of suburban employment centers is, by definition, large numbers of jobs relative to employed residents. Cervero (1989) used 1.25 as a dividing line for defining suburban communities that are predominantly job centers—what some planners call places that are jobs-rich and housing-poor. In 1990, 7 of the 18 Bay Area suburban communities with populations above 50,000 had ratios of jobs to employed-residents that exceeded 1.25: Pleasanton, Hayward, San Landry, Santa Rosa, Walnut Creek, Sunnyvale, Santa Clara, and Palo Alto. The communities with the greatest job surpluses (ratios above 1.6) were all in the Silicon Valley, the nation's premier high-technology complex: Sunnyvale, Santa Clara, and Palo Alto.

Although the emergence of suburban downtowns and edge cities have brought about more multicentered settlement patterns, these patterns do not generally follow a well-ordered central-place hierarchy. In a study of six large U.S. metropolitan regions, Pivo (1990) concluded that most office jobs were located in small- and moderate-sized, low-intensity clusters along freeway corridors. Pivo has described America's suburban structure as "The Net of Mixed Beads," an analogy to convey the reality that office complexes and employment concentrations in the suburbs come in all shapes and sizes, some still true to the classic image of low-density sprawl, some beginning to look more like compact, high-density cities (Chinitz, 1993). Gordon et al. (1986) and Giuliano and Small (1991) have likewise found that, except for several large concentrations, small-scale clustering best characterizes subcentering in the Los Angeles region. The decentralization process in contemporary urban America is complex and not easily characterized, ranging from scatteration on one extreme to more ordered, central-place type hierarchies at the other, with small-scale clustering along corridors (e.g., a net of mixed beads) occupying the middle ground.

CLASSIFYING SUBURBAN EMPLOYMENT CENTERS

In terms of the physical, land-use characteristics of suburban centers, Cervero's 1989 study of 57 large-scale suburban employment complexes in the United States remains the most comprehensive work to date. The 57 employment centers, surveyed in 1987–88, were located at least 5 radial mi (8 km) from a regional CBD and contained over 2,000 full-time workers and over 1 million ft^2 (93,000 m^2) of office space. The 57 suburban centers were drawn from 25 different metropolitan areas across the United States; most are what Garreau loosely defines as edge cities—representing, in addition to employment concentrations, centers of downtown-like activities that are outside of traditional downtowns.

Four dimensions of the land-use environment were used in the 1989 study to classify suburban centers: 1, scale; 2, density; 3, land-use composition; 4, site design. Factor analysis was used to distill the variables into the four underlying factors, and a clustering algorithm was used to group together cases along these four land-use dimensions. The 57 suburban centers were assigned to one of six different homogenous classes:

1. *Office parks*—master-planned, low-density campus-style projects (under 1,000 acres of land area) with abundant free parking and where offices occupy over 65 percent of floorspace. Ten of the 57 surveyed centers were classified office parks, including Bishop Ranch outside of San Francisco, Corporate Woods on the fringes of Kansas City, and New England Executive Park west of Boston.
2. *Office concentrations*—moderately dense, free-standing structures built independently of each other, occupying over 2 million ft^2 (0.19 million m^2) of floorspace in a well-defined geographic space; examples are Greenway Plaza near Houston and Greenwood Plaza outside of Denver.
3. *Large-scale mixed-use developments*—mixed-use concentrations that encompass 3 mi^2 (7.77 km^2) or more, containing at least one regional shopping mall representing primary growth magnets within regions. Fourteen of the 57 centers were classified as large-scale mixed-use complexes, including East Garden City on Long Island and Schaumburg Village northwest of Chicago. Garreau defined all of these as edge cities—most average far more acreage and have less of a highrise profile than inner-tier edge cities or subcities.

4. *Moderate-scale mixed-use developments*—equivalent to their larger counterparts, but averaging one-third or less acreage and generally less dense. Examples of moderate-scale mixed-use complexes are Hunt Valley north of Baltimore and the Chagrin Boulevard corridor east of Cleveland.
5. *Edge cities*—in every respect, notable for their downtown-like densities and mixed inventories of office, retail-commercial, and residential land uses. Unlike downtowns and most urban centers, however, subcities feature new buildings, wide separation between structures, new postmodern buildings, and plentiful parking. Ten subcities were identified among the 57 large centers, including Tysons Corner in northern Virginia and South Coast Metro in Orange County, California.
6. *Large-scale office corridors*—large expanses of offices and mixed-use development [50 to 100 mi^2 (129.5 to 259 km^2)] oriented along one or more freeways or major arterials, producing a distinct linear form. All are dotted by numerous office parks, industrial parks, retail centers, commercial strips, and planned urban developments. Examples of large-scale office corridors are Route 128 that rings greater Boston, Route 1 in central New Jersey, and the Silicon Valley of northern Santa Clara County.

Other researchers have subsequently developed similar profiles of suburban activity centers. The Houston Area Research Center (1989) applied the schema developed by Robert Cervero to identify 67 suburban activity centers across the United States, with 7 in the Houston region alone. In an in-depth study of travel characteristics at suburban activity centers, JHK & Associates found similar variation in office development across individual parcels in Bellevue (WA), South Coast Metro (CA), Parkway Center (TX), Perimeter Center (GA), Tysons Corner (VA), and Southdale (MN) (Hooper, 1989). Several recent studies of activity centers in greater Washington, D.C., have opted for more generic definitions. The Maryland National Capital Park and Planning Commission (1990) identified 20 activity centers with 5 million ft^2 (0.46 million m^2) of office and retail space and over 20,000 employees. Douglass (1992) more recently distinguished the region's suburban centers as belonging to one of two types: suburban campuses and suburban CBDs. Compared with Cervero's classification, suburban campuses consist mainly of office parks and some moderate-scale mixed-use developments; suburban CBDs, on the other hand, represent all other centers (e.g., office concentrations, large-scale mixed-use developments, subcities, and large-scale office corridors).

For purposes of TCRP Project B-6, a coarser but simpler schema for classifying suburban employment centers is proposed than that originally developed by Cervero:

- Suburban campuses (office parks, industrial parks, science parks),
- Edge cities (new vs. mature), and
- Suburban corridors.

This three-part breakdown reflects basic differences in major employment centers along the dimensions of scale, density, and site design. Suburban campuses are generally the smallest and the least dense. Edge cities fall in the middle in terms of size but are the densest centers. Suburban corridors encompass the most land area and have average to moderate densities. Edge cities and suburban corridors are generally mixed use in character, whereas suburban campuses feature a single predominant use. The site design characteristics of all three centers tend to be similar, featuring (by central city standards) new buildings, attractive landscaping, wide boulevards, spacious building setbacks, large supplies of surface parking, and minimal pedestrian provisions. Of courses, individual projects and sites vary considerably along these dimensions, although collectively these features reflect the strong automobile orientation of America's suburban centers.

An additional dimension that could prove useful for refining the definition of edge cities is their relative age. Some edge cities, like Stamford (CO), Bethesda (MD), and Dearborn (MI) (as defined by Garreau) are decades old, having undergone a transformation from former industrial towns to office centers. Most edge cities, however, are relatively new, having experienced the lion's share of employment growth during the office building boom of the 1980s—such as Tysons Corner (VA), Corporate Woods (MO), and Las Colinas (TX). Age could be a relevant factor in this study to the degree that older edge cities have more established transit services, different land-use mixes (e.g., more light industrial uses), fewer parking provisions, and perhaps a workforce composition (e.g., more blue-collar workers) that is more conducive to transit riding. Although the land-use makeup of employment centers is likely a more decisive factor in shaping travel behavior and service strategies, the relative age of centers is thought to be important enough to warrant some consideration in the selection of case sites.

Although most of the empirical work that has been conducted on classifying suburban centers occurred 5 to 7 years ago, these classifications remain valid today for the simple reason that little has changed. Most suburban office markets in the United States approached saturation by the late-1980s, victims of speculation (spurred on by tax policies that encouraged office overbuilding through passive write-offs and real-estate syndication), changing tax laws (that removed incentives to speculate), and a national recession. According to the Urban Land Institute (1993), the most significant recent trend in office development has been the movement of large corporations to a growth vector that has become the "favored quarter," which is nearly always in the immediate proximity of upper-middle and upper-end executive housing—for example, the north side of Dallas between Park Cities and Plano, northeast of Phoenix between the Biltmore district and Scottsdale, the east side of Seattle from Bellevue to Redmond, and the north side of metropolitan Atlanta between Buckhead and Dunwoody.

Based on recent events, Leinberger (1993) forecasts growth leapfrogging beyond these favored quarters into the exurban frontier in coming years. Leading the way have been large corporations that have moved to the outermost fringes of their respective metropolitan areas, beyond most office and industrial development of the 1980s, such as Chrysler moving its corporate headquarters to Auburn Hills 25 mi (40 km) north of downtown Detroit; Sears moving its merchandising division to Hoffman Estates, 37 mi (59.5 km) from downtown Chicago and 12 mi (19 km) farther out than Schaumburg, where much of the region's office space located during the 1980s; and J.C. Penny opening its new 2 million ft^2 (186,000 m^2) headquarters complex in Plano, 35 mi (56 km) from downtown Dallas.

As they mature, America's edge cities are increasingly being vacated by large corporations, with smaller companies taking their place. According to Faux (1994) in *The Edge City News,* there were 181 edge cities in late 1994. The top 10 areas in the United States in terms of the percentage of firms with 50 or fewer workers are all edge cities—in Buckhead (north Atlanta) and Walnut Creek (east of Oakland), 87 percent of all firms have 50 or fewer workers, the highest shares in the nation for large-scale activity centers.

Real estate market experts predict filtering in America's suburban office inventory over the next decade (Urban Land Institute, 1993). Firms in inner-tier suburban centers will tend to move into multitenant speculative space built in 1980s edge cities like Tysons Corner and Post Oak, companies will build new facilities in emerging edge cities like Leesburg, Virginia, and the Woodlands (north of Houston), and large Fortune 500 firms will venture even farther out onto the metropolitan fringes to create their own rural-like corporate havens. In light of these expected growth trends, the researchers propose a final classification of suburban employment growth: exurban corporate enclaves.

Exurban corporate enclaves mean large corporate headquarters and related ancillary uses (e.g., small retail plazas) that have sprung up in exurban and rural settings on the far fringes of metropolitan areas, such as Plano, Texas, and Hoffman Estates, Illinois.

SUMMARY ON SUBURBAN CLASSIFICATIONS

The research conducted in this appendix underscores the advantages of framing the definitions of suburban environments along physical land-use and urban form dimensions. Namely, emerging travel patterns and demands for transit services are very strongly linked to physical land-use environments. Polycentric regional structures, edge cities, and exurban corporate enclaves all pose different challenges in designing transit services, fare practices, institutional arrangements, and other programs that are responsive to consumer demand.

In summary, the following classes of suburban environments will be used in TCRP Project B-6 for structuring analysis and selecting cases:

- Residential suburbs: predominantly single-family housing,
- Residential suburbs: mixed housing,
- Balanced mixed-use suburbs,
- Suburban campuses,
- Edge cities,
- Suburban corridors, and
- Exurban corporate enclaves.

All of these represent physical land-use settings where transit services currently exist in the United States, and where, the researchers believe, lie considerable opportunities for attracting new customer bases.

Although suburban environments will be defined mainly in terms of their physical land-use makeup because of the reasonably strong correlation of built forms to travel demand, many other dimensions will be introduced and used, not to overstratify the classifications but to define the conditions of effectiveness in these suburban environments that differentiate one location from another even within a category. Such dimensions include the political-institutional environment—for example, the existence of regional transit authorities, suburban transit jurisdictions, privately provided transit services, consolidated city-county governments, proactive regional planning, or numerous political jurisdictions within a region. Other conditions of effectiveness that define variations in the categories defined above could also be their transit services and infrastructure—for example, all-rail, mixed rail-bus, mixed HOV-bus, or bus-only cities. Conditions of effectiveness also can be considered on the demand side—for example, captive vs. choice riders, geographic ridership markets (e.g., radial, reverse-commute, crosstown trip making), and peak vs. nonpeak travel. Suburban employment centers can be differentiated according to employment and occupational compositions.

To begin classifying suburban dimensions along these additional dimensions and creating subclassifications for each of the seven categories would introduce considerable complexity and quite likely overload the research design.

Therefore, the researchers rely mainly on the seven land-use-related classes of suburban environments, using the research results to provide insights into the degree to which some of these other dimensions of the suburban transportation environment affect suburban transit programs.